PATHFYNDER

PATHFYNDER

---

*How I Use Personal Courage
and Emotional Control to
Face Fear, Build Success,
and Get What I Want*

ERINN WATKINS

Eric Watkins

Verdelite Publishing, LLC

ENDORSEMENTS

A word I would use to describe Erinn's story is Defiant! She cracked the code early with understanding and knowing her self-worth and not letting anyone take that away from her. She describes in detail, toxic leaders and how a negative command culture can be created from it. She takes you on a journey of her decision making in not only dealing with horrible leadership, but how she chose to move on into career fields where many would dare to explore and very few women have succeeded. Her writing skills are introduced early on in her journey, and she uses them throughout in various situations helping others through challenging leadership which paved the way for others behind her. She has a road map to dealing with mental health issues and challenged herself to stay on the road to becoming the best version of herself. I am very proud of MSG Erinn Watkins and honored that our paths crossed at National Guard Bureau (NGB). She was a force to be reckoned with then and has found a way to be a force to be reckoned with now. While the situations she was placed in are unfortunate and should never happen to anyone, she has shown why tenacity and resilience are so critically important and I believe her story and accomplishments will help so many to follow.

I highly encourage everyone to purchase and read her story, in it you will find the leader that you want to be and learn from leadership you will want to avoid. You will also find through her tenacity, how to navigate your own mine fields and become the best version of yourself when others doubt you.

Victor Angry
United States Army Command Sergeant Major (CSM), Retired
Former Army National Guard CSM (2009). National Guard Bureau
Neabsco District Supervisor
Prince William County Board of County Supervisors

Erinn Watkins pours her soul out while defending this grateful nation, this book is a must-read if you lose a sense of direction, This book will instill confidence, and hope where in the reader where it may be difficult to find.

Mario L. Barber
United States Army Sergeant Major, Retired, 30 years of services

Write a review!

Book Cover by Eric Watkins
Left: SGT Erinn Watkins, 1st BN, 507th IN (ABN), Ft Benning, GA
Right: MSG Erinn Watkins, National Guard Bureau, Arlington, VA

ISBN: 979-8-9885185-0-1 - paperback
ISBN: 979-8-9885185-1-8 - ebook

First Printing, 2023
Verdelite Publishing, LLC
www.verdelitepublishing.com

Send all publishing inquiries including permission for reprints and excerpts, contact verdelitepublishing@pm.me.

Author Website: www.ErinnSpeaks.com

To my son, Eric—

This is the story of how we got through it.

To my sister, Erica—

Thank you for listening to my strategies and being supportive.

In Remembrance:

Major Martin Lee Sharber
Tennessee Army National Guard, Retired

LET'S CONNECT

*Let's make sure we stay in touch!
Please visit my website to connect, find out the latest,
and for more information on upcoming books in the
PathfYnder series:*

www.erinnspeaks.com

Or Email me at info@erinnspeaks.com

CONTENTS

8 Working on My Best Self 73

9 The Final Straw 87

10 Mental Health Challenges 99

11 Attempting to Survive Fort Bragg 118

12 Post-Military Life 130

Epilogue 141
Acknowledgements 145
About The Author 147
A History of Success 149
Photo Gallery 161
Glossary 169
References And Credits 171
Verdelite Publishing, LLC 173

DISCLAIMER

The publisher and the author are providing this book and its contents on an "as is" basis and make no representations or warranties of any kind with respect to this book or its contents and disclaim all such representations and warranties, including but not limited to warranties of mental health care for a particular purpose.

The content of this book is for informational purposes only and is not intended to diagnose, treat, cure, or prevent any mental condition or disease. This book is not intended as a substitute for consultation with a licensed practitioner. Please consult with a physician or health-care specialist regarding the suggestions and recommendations made in this book.

While this book is not a work of fiction. any names. events. or incidents which could damage the legitimate reputations of persons in good standing characters have been stricken from the record or modified. Any resemblance to actual persons, living or dead, or actual events is purely coincidental.

AUTHOR'S NOTE

Race and sex are provided for context and are not meant to imply racism or sexism.

QUOTES

*"**Courage is a moral quality**; it is not a chance gift of nature like an aptitude for games.*
*It is a cold choice between two alternatives, the fixed resolve not to quit; an act of renunciation which must be made not once but many times by the power of the will. **Courage is will power.**"*
- The Anatomy Of Courage By Lord Moran (Page 61) -

*"A sender with no receiver is just **a noise maker**."*

- Erinn Watkins -

"She's so centered in how intelligent she is that she doesn't necessarily think of herself as a woman first...she just automatically assumes shes' equal."
- Anya Taylor-Joy, The Queen's Gambit -

"If you want to change the world, you must be your very best in the darkest moments."
- Admiral William H. McRaven -

"the real self is dangerous..., because once a man knows his real self, he becomes an individual."
- Meditation, THE FIRST and LAST FREEDOM, A Practical Guide to OSHO Meditations -

MY PHILOSOPHY

- Stop taking ownership of things that don't belong you.

- Be patient.

- Have faith in yourself and your abilities.

- Live well. Be your best self.

- Learn how to take a joke.

- Recognize sarcasm.

- Smile, even when you don't want to.

- Know when to take the hit.

- Ask for help and learn to accept help.

- When you choose your path, you get everything that goes with it.

- Don't dwell on the why. It's not as important as the what.

- Identify action items.

- Majority positions are not always correct. Learn to stand alone.

- Think outside the box.

- Assume the positive...only the first time.

- Never go along to get along.

- Understand where people are coming from.

- You don't always have to be right.

- Focus more on commonalities instead of differences.

- Everything does not deserve an answer.

- Everyone does not deserve an apology.

- Everything is not an insult.

SIMPLE & PLAIN

I believe that each man should stand by his conviction, regardless of the consequence that stands before one.

For if you budge a single inch from the true desire of your heart, you then have been forced to live a lie.

So if the question is put before you, how far will you go for what you believe in...so strongly that your direction cannot be changed, confess this to your spirit and you will find your physical actions to be on the same parallel.

I believe it is time to give of ourselves so that another will know he is cared for and, in return, your welfare will be another's concern.

I believe it is time to remove the so called dignity of vengeance to prepare the way for an extra effort to understand the Human Being.

I want to love and not hate.

I'd rather help than obstruct.

I want to be a significant part of the reason for a smile on someone's face.

And if I should be so lucky, let me be instrumental in removing the painful frown another may bear.

This is the road I choose to travel...the road that has been paved with footprints to follow.

So if the question is put before me, "How far would I go for what I believe in?"

I would have to say,

All the way, All the way.

By the Human Mind

PREFACE

Why is *Pathfynder* spelled with a Y?

Y stands for Decision Point - Your path comes to a fork in the road where you can go left or right. The Pathfynder Principle will allow you to pick one so you can move forward, make a decision and stand by it, and deal with any repercussions that may come. The Pathfynder Principle is about acceptance and controlling your emotions so you can always get what you want.

What is the Pathfynder Principle?

1) The Pathfynder Principle begins with acknowledging the situation you're in. This is your Decision Point. This forces you to be honest with yourself. Once you acknowledge your circumstances, you then either accept them in their current form or you make micro-agreements to help move you to the path you want to take. Make as many micro-agreements as necessary to help move you to your next Decision Point.

2) Turn off your emotions. Recognize blockages, triggers and address them. Separate feelings from facts. Identify things you can control. Recognize when you're anxious about something that hasn't happened yet. If it's not here yet, then you're thinking too far ahead. Find your Step 1.

3) Take action and stand by it. This is how you get on the off-ramp. Using your micro-agreements, just do it. Don't think about it. If one micro-agreement is to walk to the corner, repeat this micro-agreement to yourself until you can take action. Once you get to the corner, look around and see what else you can do. This is your next micro-agreement. Repeat each micro-agreement as necessary until you can move to the next one. Repeat step 2.

What you will read in Pathfynder.

1) Personal stories that illustrate where I failed at first in being aware of the Pathfynder Principle.

2) Stories of how I discovered the Pathfynder Principle and how it began to work for me.

3) Multiple uses of how the Pathfynder Principle can work for you.

PROLOGUE

My Last Day in the Military

I felt so angry, disgusted, and betrayed. Here I was, United States Army Master Sergeant Erinn Watkins with twenty-nine years of service to my country, being escorted through the hallways and out the building I once worked in.

I was being thrown away like yesterday's garbage. Everything I had worked for, suffered through, and accomplished was for nothing. I was no longer needed, and it had been made clear long before this day came that I was not appreciated. The Army had turned its back on me.

Before I even reached the door to the outside, I was boiling on the inside. But no one knew it because I kept it bottled up where no one could see it (as usual). Despite it all, I was defiant. I knew I would find a way to get through the situation.

I was being escorted by one of the Soldiers who worked in the Orderly Room, which was standard procedure, especially considering the building was a high security area. Unlike the others, he was helpful and kind. We chatted a little bit as we made our way from one floor to the next as I out-processed. Then it was over. All I needed was to pick up my discharge paperwork, which included my DD214 (Certificate of Release or Discharge from Active Duty).

On my way to the Soldier Support Center (also known as the "Soldier Neglect Center"), I passed a female Lieutenant Colonel in the hallway. We chatted for a moment, and before we parted ways, she looked at me and said, "Regulations are for people who follow them." How profound that was to me at that moment! She knew, as I did, that this is how the game is played. It's nothing personal.

When it was my turn, my name was called and I went into a back office. The woman who finalized my paperwork was pleasant and straightforward. I signed where she told me to sign. Then she gave me the all too familiar parting gift. It was a black and yellow box with the US Army logo on the front. I'd seen it before. It's the same box given to other Soldiers at their retirement ceremonies, but I didn't expect to receive mine in such an unceremonious manner. Opening it in front of me, she explained its contents: a neatly folded US flag, an ink pen, a US Army sticker, and a standard "thank you" letter.

Then she gave me my retirement certificate. I looked at it and saw that it was signed by someone I didn't know. I didn't want it. She could have kept everything, and I wouldn't have cared. Even the flag. At that point, the only thing that was important to me was my DD214. I had been in my career for my entire adult life, and without my deserved retirement ceremony, the contents of the box were meaningless. I had no use for anything the Army had to give me, but I took it because she was just doing her job and there was no need to take it out on her. Then it was over.

No retirement ceremony, no award. Just a certificate and a push out the door. While a lot of young girls dream of their wedding day, I dreamed about my retirement ceremony. I fought so hard to just make it to eighteen years. Because at eighteen years, I knew I was locked in for twenty. There was nothing they could do to me to change that. Once I made it to eighteen, I thought it would be smooth sailing, but it wasn't. I never received my retirement ceremony. I never received a retirement award.

Despite the continued hostility and conflict in my last three years of service, I still had the audacity to dream about my retirement ceremony. Who would I invite? What food would I serve? What would I say? What kind of gifts would I receive? I thought my day was coming, but it never did.

Suddenly, it hit me like a ton of bricks. All that I had refused to let myself feel burst inside me and I couldn't hide it anymore. My fight was over. The woman in the out-processing office gave me a tremendous hug, which was something I needed and accepted. I had spent so much time trying to be in control of my life and my entire career that I had forgotten what it felt like to be cared for.

I took my flag in a box and my certificate and went home. Once I was alone, I committed one final act of defiance. I decided that I would close the door on all of it. So, everything I wore that last day of service went into a garbage bag.

This book is the story of how I reframed my thoughts about my service.

| 1 |

On My Own

My story begins in my childhood with my parents and sister, who is two years older than I am. One of my earliest memories is having a birthday cake when I turned five years old. It wasn't a birthday party in the sense that other children were there to celebrate with me. Ironically enough, that birthday cake was the only "birthday" I ever remember celebrating because it was also the last one I celebrated with my family.

I grew up in the projects of New Orleans with parents who were dysfunctional and argued a lot. There was a lot of conflict and hostility between them. My parents ended up divorcing when Erica, my sister, and I were very young, and she and I did a lot of bouncing back and forth between both of their families, even though they lived in the very same projects, in buildings that were right next to each other. We still played with the same cousins of both families.

Out of both of my parents, my mother's involvement—rather lack of involvement—in our lives is one of her most perplexing characteristics. To sum it up, my mother just wasn't concerned about us. She didn't act like a mother, and Erica and I couldn't rely on her like children rely on on their mothers.

For example, my mother would entertain people at all hours of the night when we were young. Once, when I was probably four or five, I had just taken a bath, and my mother had company over. When I finished, she asked me to come into the living room so she could get me dressed. Instead of coming to me to dress me, I had to come to her and be dressed in front of a group of adults that included men as well as women. I cried my eyes out. Even as a little child, I knew there was something wrong about that.

My mom didn't protect me, and she didn't seem to care about me or where I was. When I was in first grade, I had an assignment to color a picture once. My teacher wouldn't let me leave until I was finished. Once I was done, I went outside to catch my bus but it had already left. I didn't worry about it, though. I could just walk home.

As I was walking along the busy streets of New Orleans, a police officer saw me, a little child, walking by myself and picked me up. Kind as he was, he brought me to his house and fed me spaghetti and salad. After dinner, he took me home. When I walked into the house, my mother looked up to see me and acted as if nothing had happened. No wondering where I had been or feeling worried for my safety. That's the kind of mother I had.

Though she recognized that my sister and I were a part of her life, she made decisions based on what she wanted from life rather than what was best for us. She wanted to escape from my dad, so we moved around a lot, which meant I attended a lot of different schools. She would always tell us that my dad would find us and that was why we would have to move again. But it didn't make any sense to us. My dad wasn't doing anything to us that was inappropriate or that made it necessary for us to move and hide from him as often as we did.

To try to make sense of all of this confusion, she would slander our dad to us. In fact, they both always "told on each other" to my sister and me, as though we would take one side over the other. But it went in one ear and out the other. Even though we were roughly eight and ten, Erica and I didn't believe the rumors from either parent.

As children, we ended up taking care of each other because they weren't doing it. At the time, that sort of dysfunction didn't register as abnormal because it was normal for us. There were no other patterns outside of the dysfunction that showed us anything different than what we were living. Moving around and going from house to house was just normal. Being poor was normal. Drinking powdered milk and eating ketchup sandwiches, syrup sandwiches, and butter and sugar sandwiches was normal.

Our normal changed slightly when my mother joined the military, and we moved to Germany. Once we were overseas, it was easy for my mother to escape my dad. I started fifth grade in my sixth elementary school when we arrived—but we finally had some stability. We stayed in Germany for the rest of my elementary years, three years of middle school, and one year of high school.

But, other than no longer moving around so often, our life in Germany was no better. Erica and I still ended up taking care of ourselves. After school, we participated in extracurricular activities that kept us out of the house for as long as possible. I ended up playing softball and volleyball and running track, Erica played basketball, and we both joined a dance team called the Heidelberg Lionettes. We used to hang out at the DYA and go to these dance events for dependent youth called "All Area" dances. The DYA, Dependent Youth Activities, was the military dependent's recreation authority, which provided recreational facilities and services for dependent youth of US military stationed in Germany. I used to read encyclopedias and phone books for fun and taught myself piano as a way to keep myself occupied. Erica and I even joined a gospel choir for children. Luckily for us, friends and neighbors "adopted" us, taking up some of my mother's slack.

When she was home, my mother didn't treat us like her children; she treated us like her personal errand runners. But I always liked going to the Shoppette. My mother gave me the money to buy what was needed, and, if I had quarters in the change, I would stop by the bowling alley to play video games. I was really good at Donkey Kong, Galaga, and Dragon Slayer. But this didn't last very long because she soon noticed that she was missing some of her change and that I was taking too long to come home, and I got in trouble.

It wasn't rare for me to get in trouble, even when I didn't do anything wrong. I was the youngest, and when we were much older, Erica told me that she noticed that my mother was particularly abusive toward me, and the abuse took the form of physical aggression. For some reason my mother took a lot of her frustrations out on me. Maybe it was because I reminded her of my father since I look just like him (and my sister looks like her).

We eventually moved to Arizona when I was in high school, and the abuse didn't subside. My mother didn't even buy food for us. One day I was heating up a microwave meal, and without saying a word, she immediately took the meal out of the microwave and put it in the garbage. Once Erica was old enough, she got a job so that we could have some food. Before that happened, one of Erica's friends would sneak us food.

Finally, Erica had enough, and we coordinated with our father for him to buy me a plane ticket so I could go live with him in New Orleans. Erica and I made it look like I ran away from home—but she got me out of there.

My time with my dad was much better than with my mother, but it wasn't perfect. In terms of personality, I'm more like my dad. He was stubborn, and I'm similarly stubborn, especially when I know I'm right. I identified more with how my dad acted because he is very intelligent.

We didn't really argue growing up, though we did have intense discussions, which helped me learn to stand on my beliefs.

As part of that process, I lost most of the intense discussions we had. When I did win, it was a wonderful feeling of accomplishment. That same feeling is what orients me as an adult when I'm making decisions or when I'm going through difficulties. Ultimately, I learned to trust myself, believe what I know, and stick with it.

Now, that's not to say that all was rosy between my dad and me. The relationship could be stressful. He was very paranoid and thought people were out to get him. That caused him to distrust me, even though I hadn't done anything to deserve that distrust. I didn't go anywhere, and I didn't have many close friends. I could not understand his paranoia, which runs in my family among my paternal uncles, and I didn't know what to do with it. I did my best to gain his approval, but nothing I did was ever enough. Though he was in the Air Force for a few years, I don't think his paranoia stems from his time in the military.

I don't remember my dad being abusive toward me, but as I got older into my teenage years, I didn't know what to do about his mental health issues, which were getting worse.

For example, he would put masking tape over all the outlets in the house because he thought people were watching him through the holes. I eventually learned how to talk to him despite his paranoia, but I didn't know how to do that as a child.

When people hear about my time growing up, they tell me that I'm strong. But I didn't realize or consider myself to be that strong as a child. I just thought I was doing what needed to be done.

I was surviving. If things went wrong, Erica and I would just fix them. We were the decision-makers. We would figure out whatever we needed to, and ultimately, we would take care of it. I'm that way to this day. If something happens, I look at it, figure it out, make a decision, and stick with it. Even if it's not the best decision, I stand by it. I would deal with any repercussions later. I used this trait in the military and as a parent.

In the military

This learned decisiveness transferred over into my military service where I learned to do a similar thing: help make decisions when others wouldn't.

For instance, once I was in PLDC on a road march. PLDC, Primary Leadership Development Course, was the first leadership course an Army soldier attends once being promoted to SPC/E4. As we got closer to our encampment, one of the instructors "killed off" the squad leader and put me in charge. He then killed off two other soldiers just as we approached a road with an encampment on the other side. Because I knew we couldn't just cross the road, I put two Soldiers on guard at either end on our side of the road. I immediately assumed that I was supposed to transport the two dead soldiers with their weapons and equipment, but the instructors didn't tell me how to do it. I decided to strip them of their gear. I tasked two other soldiers to carry the casualties. I had all four weapons on "stacked arms" and put a guard on them with the gear. In my mind, it was easier to carry soldiers without gear than with it. I happened to glance at the instructors and they were amazed at what I was doing. But I got it done. I attribute problem-solving like this to making decisions at an early age and sticking to them.

In the military, we called this "making a command decision." I had to learn to be tactical in this ability because I didn't want to be perceived as someone who usurps others' authority, not in front of subordinates and not among colleagues, even if they trusted my judgment and leadership more. So, I had to be a good follower.

There were times I've had some valuable input to offer a leader that could make a difference to others. But I wouldn't want to take over as if I were challenging the leader's authority. I would make suggestions to the leader and let them lead. It was up to them whether they would accept my advice.

As a parent

When I became a parent, I distinctly remember wanting to break the cycle and not wanting to continue the same dysfunction I had growing up because it didn't work for me. I didn't want to repeat it. This was a decision I made that I didn't go back on.

When my son, Eric, was younger, I would see a problem and fix it. Once he was old enough, I started to change my approach with him. I wanted him to be as self-sufficient as possible, to use his own judgment based on the guidance I had given him and the examples I had already set. I didn't make a habit of telling him what to do if I didn't have to. Rather, I would "highly suggest" or "highly recommend" certain things. I would merely make suggestions and follow it up with, "but you can do what you want." Ultimately it would be his decision. He usually followed my advice. Even as he got older, he would still call me to ask for my advice. I have always wanted to maintain an open line of communication with him.

There were also times when I'd see things that needed to be done and would just go ahead and do them. You can't always wait on someone else. That was also part of making decisions as a child: standing by them and trusting in myself. I never questioned myself.

I encourage parents not to be afraid of letting their children make mistakes and to let their children fix their mistakes on their own. When Eric went off to college, he would call me and tell me about some situation he was dealing with. I remember patiently waiting for him to ask for my help. And when he didn't, I had to let him be a man and handle his own business. This is how they learn a lot of life's lessons. How many decisions can a child make that meet the criteria of life and death? When your children do make mistakes that bother you but don't rise to the occasion of a felony, don't get too excited.

So, while I wish I'd had a different childhood, I am grateful for how it shaped me to be a better soldier and mother.

| 2 |

Be All You Can Be

I was a fast learner in high school. My sister always knew that I was smart, although I never did. I just knew school was something I had to do. It was a requirement: I had to go to this place and do this work, and they were going to give me a grade. It just so happened that most of my grades were As, but I didn't have to work at it. Excelling in schoolwork was normal for me, and every year, I took my rightful place in mostly honors and advance placement classes. Thinking back on this, I realize how important that has been to me in practice. Intellectual intelligence played a huge role in helping me figure out my emotional intelligence and how to navigate life issues without having someone to talk to about them.

None of what I was learning in school was ever challenging, and there was no one who really pushed me to do my best, but I did the work because I was responsible and felt obligated to do what was required of me.

When I graduated from my fifth high school in three years, I decided to stay local, despite receiving many college offers, and attend Southern University at New Orleans to study computer science. When I signed up for college algebra, it was so easy that I requested to take the final on the second day of class and passed. I finished in two semesters.

Just as with high school, college was not challenging. I did find solace, though, by taking a world history course. I've always been interested in how things began and how everything is connected, so I find history fascinating.

Later on, I somehow got the idea that I wanted to go to the Air Force Academy in order to fly jets. As a part of the entry process, I had to put a packet together that involved school transcripts, test scores, a recommendation letter from my senator, and a physical among a number of things.

During that process, I found out that I had seven wisdom teeth and was told they all needed to be pulled before I could go. Because my dad couldn't afford that much dental work, and because I had no other way to pay for it, I joined the military to get the dental work done for free.

At that time, I was staying with my dad, but once I joined the military, I ended up closing the door on the relationship with him. I felt it necessary to do so because having a relationship with him was simply not helpful.

People find it difficult to separate personal maturity from the "honoring" of parents. But, sometimes family relationships aren't helpful no matter how much anyone tries to convince you otherwise. When my mother was off on her own and when I left my father, I was making a statement: that I would take full responsibility for myself. And though I had done that to some extent as a little child, I could finally do it for real by putting distance between us.

But I couldn't detach from the effects of having lived with him. At basic in training, I was having nightmares that my dad was chasing me. When I left him, I was trying to escape. In the dream, I would be running down the same street in New Orleans where I was raised. As soon as I would hit the corner, I'd wake up in terror. One day, I decided that I wasn't going to run anymore. And that in the dream, I decided to face him. So in the same dream when I got to the corner, I turned around to face him. Then I woke up. I never had that same dream again.

I believe that I was having those dreams because I was still trying to escape from him emotionally even though he wasn't with me.

Start of my military career

I joined the Army Reserves. With the dreams gone, basic training ended up being the break I needed and a lot of fun. I had seen a lot of movies about basic training in high school like Full Metal Jacket, so I had an idea of how it might be. The women had to do three push-ups in order to get out of reception. This is where I learned I had good upper body strength.

After that, they took us by bus to the barracks. The Drill Sergeants gave us one trip to exit the bus carrying all of our belongings and make it into the open bay barracks to stand by our bunks. They came upstairs and yelled, "Stand by your bunks!" A very aggressive male Drill Sergeant walked down the aisle, yelling at each of us one by one. I was the last one in my row, and as I glanced down the aisle, I knew my turn was coming.

When he got to me, I couldn't believe it. He was as short as I was—and I'm short! He defied every stereotype I had of Hollywood's version of a Drill Sergeant. When he got nose to nose with me, yelling in my face, I couldn't help laughing. He made me drop and do push-ups on the spot. I never made fun of him again.

I enjoyed doing different things and learning about a lot of topics that were new to me. For basic training, we had Army Reserve Drill Sergeants. So, every two weeks, we would have a change of command, which always kept things new and exciting. One time, we had a female Drill Sergeant, which was pretty neat because you didn't really get to see that too much.

Basic training was also the place where I was able to shine. I learned some things about myself. One skill I was naturally good at was drill and ceremony (or D&C as we called it). I also learned that I was good at details and organization

I remember the first time I held a weapon: we were all lined up next to the Armor Room, and one by one we were issued our weapons, an M16A1 for each of us. As soon as I got it in my hands and stepped out the door, I began crying. I was holding something that killed people. That realization hit me like a ton of bricks.

The Drill Sergeant asked, "What's the matter with you, private?"

"Nothing, Drill Sergeant," I said. I sucked it up and carried on. I got over it.

When it was time for us to go to the gas chamber, there was a lot of talk about it that week. My buddies were very worried about what was going to happen. Maybe the Drill Sergeants had pumped our heads with scary stories, but they didn't faze me.

The day of the gas chamber, we were out in the field and the chamber was actually just a small, one-room building in the middle of nowhere. We were lined up to go in, and I was in front. We had already done some pre-training, donned our masks, and sealed them. We were ready to go.

Standing in line with our masks on, I led our group into the dimly lit building. There was a Drill Sergeant in the far corner with his mask on, standing behind a barrel with smoke coming out of it. I walked all the way to the other side of the room where there was the exit door and another Drill Sergeant. Then we all turned to face the front and were given several commands to execute: unseal and reseal our masks. Things went fine. The final command was to remove our masks, state our names, then WALK out the exit door.

I took my mask off and, for some unknown reason, I took a breath of air. Immediately, I started coughing and ran for the door. The Drill Sergeant wrapped his arms around me, swung me back into the room and shouted, "WALK, Private!" I knew right then what I needed to do to get out of that room. I walked outside and started laughing. That's why there's a picture of me in our basic training yearbook laughing as I was coming out of the gas chamber. I was laughing because I should have walked and because it really was not all it was cracked up to be. It wasn't that bad.

When I finished basic, I went to my first Advanced Individual Training (AIT) where I was an Administrative Specialist. When I took the Armed Services Vocational Aptitude Battery (ASVAB), I had scored high enough to pick any job I wanted. Even though I was estranged from my mother at the time (who was still in the military), I still took her recommendation to go into Admin (71L) which was her MOS, military occupational specialty.

The most memorable thing about AIT at Fort Jackson was that my leadership skills developed on road marches where I was assigned as a Road Guard. At first, no one wanted to be a Road Guard because that meant you had to do a lot of running. The responsibility of the Road Guards was to block traffic at every cross street as we were marching from one place to another. When it became my turn to be a Road Guard, I decided that us Road Guards needed to look more professional. I came up with a routine we would do as each Road Guard was relieved during the formation. The two Road Guards in the front would run up to an intersection, then get into a modified parade rest position with the left arm behind the back and the right arm outstretched to block traffic. As soon as the two Road Guards in the front took off running, the two in the rear of the formation took off as well to meet them at the same intersection. They would stand behind those two, at the position of attention, and tap their shoulder. The first two did an about face and saluted each other, and then took off running to catch up to the front of the formation. It worked so well that people started volunteering, and we had to have tryouts to see who could make the team.

After all the success and enjoyment I had while I was away in training, once it was over, I went back home to my dad. I discovered that his paranoia had not improved and my only option was to go active duty to get away from home. A week before my ship date, I actually moved into a hotel and rented a car just so I could be away. I left for my second AIT, which was 76C (Equipment Records and Parts Specialist).

First duty station

My first duty station was Fort Hood at the 2nd Armored Division: "Hell on Wheels." Of all the memories I have from Fort Hood, the one that sticks out is when we had to do these events called the Corps Run. In the Corps Run, there were all the major commands that fell under III Corps. Each command or company had their own formation (we lined up based on height), and together we made up one massive formation. Each company had cadence callers who ran at the back of the company and would take turns relieving the person calling the cadence. We would run together throughout the post, which was usually five miles. One of the things the male soldiers did was take the guidon which was at the front with the Commander, the higher the unit, the bigger and heavier the guidon. Someone from the formation would run up, take the guidon, run to the back of the entire company formation, run around the back of the formation back to the front and hand it back to the guidon bearer who ran next to the Commander.

I thought that feat was so awesome, but I didn't realize how difficult it was until I tried it. When I would watch the males do it, it was so motivating. Everybody would be cheering them on as they took the guidon, held it up in the air, and ran around the whole formation. No matter where you were in formation, you could see it.

Once I got to a point where I had built up my run, I felt that I was ready to do it. As the shortest person, I was already in the front row, so I didn't have to run far to get the guidon. Once I got it, I was committed to the task and ran all the way to the back, which was pretty easy because you're only running in the opposite direction of the formation. But then you have to round the back of the formation and begin running the same direction, but faster so you can get back to the front. That's where you find out what you're made of.

It was hard, but I had no choice. I was committed. I was going to get this guidon around this formation and get it back to the Commander. And, you know, that was probably one of the first strong senses of physical accomplishment that I could recall in my life up until that time.

This desire to be the best I could be stayed with me throughout my entire career.

| 3 |

Everything Falls Apart

Fort Hood is where I was stationed when we got involved with the first war, Desert Shield.

I was working in the motor pool with my company, and I noticed pretty quickly that the Army was picking people from my company one by one to make up a larger unit to go on deployment. I remember when they took my sergeant. Then they took my squad leader. They were taking key people who were critical to our success as a unit and also critical to our ability to function as a section. We had the same amount of work between fewer people. Our responsibilities didn't change, so we had to make it work and it was very stressful.

After Fort Hood, I went to Germany before eventually going on to Fort Benning. When I was stationed in Germany, I had an unintentional pregnancy. It never occurred to me to not have my child, even though his father wasn't involved, which left me in a difficult spot, but I knew that I would handle whatever came my way regardless of how difficult —just as I have done my entire life. In a way, this was me making a statement that I was responsible for this little person who I brought into the world.

At the time, I was going through a number of things that made that time in my life very hard. I was ready to leave my unit because it had turned into an environment that was hostile and there was a lot of conflict. I was six-months pregnant, and they wanted me to perform weapons training, lying on my belly on a concrete floor. I was not going to do that. I needed to escape this unit, but having a child meant that I would need to stay in Germany for longer. Having a dependent meant that my overseas tour would be changed from unaccompanied for two years to accompanied for three years. This was automatic. I didn't want to do that, but I found out that in order for me to leave Germany on my scheduled departure date, Eric would have to be at least two months old in order to fly or else I'd be extended one year. He was two months and two days old when we left Germany.

By the time Eric was born, his father had moved from Germany. Believe it or not, I was never able to find him to let him know that he was the father. I looked for him, but it ended up being futile because I didn't have his name right. I knew his mother's name (or I thought I knew his mother's name), and I knew he was from Chattanooga. I named my son after my sister and gave him my last name. His middle name came to me as I was watching the movie Glory with Denzel Washington.

I received orders to go to Fort Sam Houston, Texas, but as a SPC/E4, I decided I didn't want to go to Texas. For one thing, I didn't want to have to drive across Texas any time I wanted to visit home in New Orleans. No one was allowed to say no to an assignment, but I'd find a way around it. I'd figure it out. So I took permanent change of station (PCS) leave (official time off between a change in duty stations) when I left Germany and went to Atlanta and stayed with Erica. Somewhere along the way, I got this idea that I could just go to the nearest Army base and sign in. Fort Benning was the closest base, so I went there and signed in off leave. Once I signed in as an "unexpected arrival," command at Fort Benning had to find a place for me to be assigned. In order for them to have to time to figure out where to put me, I was able to take Permissive TDY, which is ten days off for house hunting. During this time, I had hopes of getting a decision that allowed me to stay there, but it actually took longer. It took an additional two weeks of my three-month-old son and me staying in an on-base hotel, which I had to pay for out of pocket before I finally received my orders assigning me to 1st Battalion, 507th Infantry (Airborne).

I knew nothing about the Airborne School or about jumping out of planes, but I didn't have to in order to be assigned there. I was assigned as an Administrative Specialist in the S-1 shop.

While working in the S-1 shop, the Battalion Sergeant Major, Sgt. Maj. "Bull Dog" McCoy, found out that I was a "leg" (a person who is non–Airborne-qualified) and wouldn't talk to me. Even though I worked in the S-1 shop, anytime he needed something he would just write me a note or send me an email. It didn't bother me at all. I just did my job. He wasn't the only one who treated me this way. For some unknown reason, the Battalion secretary never liked me. One day, she told me to my face, "I'll see to it that you never go to PLDC and you'll never go to Airborne School." But she was just a secretary. What made her think she had that much pull? I didn't give it too much thought. Unfortunately, I continued to run into people who treated me poorly throughout my career. This was just the start. But despite it all, I always worked on being my best self.

Being my best self

One of my responsibilities while working in the S-1 shop was to manage Soldier/Non-Commissioned Officer (NCO) of the Month Boards and formal promotion boards. The Soldier/NCO of the Month Boards were, in essence, practice for the promotion board. A soldier or NCO had to demonstrate military knowledge, bearing, and professionalism, all while presenting themselves in their dress uniform before a panel of senior NCOs. You knew the topics covered but not which questions each board member would ask you. You competed with several other soldiers or NCOs, and the one who performed the best was awarded Soldier or NCO of the Month. This winner would then go on to compete at higher levels, building up to the Soldier or NCO of the Installation. This sort of recognition usually led to other outstanding achievements.

One of the things I did in conducting these boards was a "uniform check." On the day of the board (if the soldier agreed), I would give their uniform a once-over to make sure they were perfect. I usually found something that they missed. One deficiency I did usually find was when I told them to open their jacket. This is something that the President of the Board would always ask them to do in order to check their "gig line." This was how the crease on their shirts lined up with the edge of their belts. Everything had to be perfect. As soon as I asked them to open their jacket, there it was: a dry-cleaning tag. It hardly ever failed.

During this time, when the Airborne Instructors, or Black Hats, came to the S-1 shop they would ask when I was coming to their company for Airborne training. I had news for them because I wasn't about to jump out of anybody's perfectly good airplane. I wore my beret and my Airborne tab as part of the unit's uniform and I was content.

PLDC was next for me. PLDC was the first leadership school a Soldier attended as an E-4 back then. Before I went to training, a female Sergeant in my company told me to raise my hand and volunteer first. I had no idea why, but I did it, thinking that she was giving me some good advice to help me through the training. My name was called and I was the first platoon sergeant. What was good about this was that I had the opportunity to lead the way for the rest of the soldiers who became leaders after me. I set the tone. I set the standard for the rest to follow.

I discovered my true leadership potential, and I was very good at it. I would have never known this had I not been put in that position. I was a natural. I was not only able to lead my platoon, but I was also good at calling cadence. Little did I know that I had a strong, powerful voice. I had about three or four cadences that I called, one right after the other. I could flow from one to the next without skipping a beat. It was as if I had my own "remix." I would call and they would answer. After my leadership position was over, I got requests to come up and call cadence for my platoon. I gladly obliged.

During the training, I found myself competing with a male corporal for the top graduate. I only knew it because one of the small group instructors told me. It didn't concern me. I was confident that I just needed to do my usual thing. If I was first, great. If I was second, that was great, too. Regardless, I was going to be at the top of the class.

The trouble begins

PLDC started off great, but then trouble found me. One night, a female student approached me and asked if I wanted to go out with an instructor from another platoon. I felt like that was the oddest thing for her to ask me. Was this a test? Was she kidding?

There were probably other females who said "yes." They were probably weak-minded, didn't know their value, didn't care, or maybe thought they could gain an unfair advantage by sleeping with the instructor. People like that are betting that you will say yes as well.

So, I told this student no without thinking twice. It was wrong and against the rules. But I learned that you don't say "no" because you'll learn to regret it.

The instructor who wanted me to "go out" with him had me called into the Commander's office because he said I had "disrespected" him.

He told the Commander that I had disrespected him in the mess hall. That was an outright lie because I had never before interacted with him. And I wasn't even a combative, outwardly emotional person. That isn't my personality. As I entered the room, I saw him, my squad leader, and the Commander. Each was telling me that I did this thing. I finally asked my accuser.

"Well, what did I say if I said something to you?"

"Well, I don't remember, but you said something," he said back.

My Company Commander and the rest of my Chain of Command actually came over (my unit was in the same vicinity) to speak on my behalf. I didn't realize how huge that was then, but I get it now what an honor it was to have my entire Chain of Command vouch for me. (My Company Commander later wrote me a note of support regarding the incident. He was sent away after that.)

Their vouching for me didn't work to salvage my outstanding performance in leadership school. I was crushed. I was given a counseling statement for this "infraction" that never occurred. I lost all accolades: the Commandant's list and the Distinguished Honor Graduate that I had earned.

Even though this situation was demoralizing, I learned how to still be my best self despite all that had happened. I was really good at calling cadence, and I was a pro at marching the platoon and squad around wherever we needed to go. When it was time to graduate, I got the bright idea to volunteer as Adjutant at the graduation ceremony, even though I wasn't getting an award. That meant that I was in charge of the whole ceremony. It was my responsibility to ensure that the company was formed and in proper alignment throughout. I did this by being posted directly on the field and shouting commands to each company. I had to speed walk onto the field. Once in position, I would yell, "Battalion, bring your units to attention and parade rest!" and so on and so forth.

The thought of having all eyes on me was powerful. I could feel the tension. The school leadership was so afraid that I was going to mess it up on purpose because of what had happened earlier. I didn't care because I knew I was going to do a good job. At the request of the other students, I ended up marching the whole company to the graduation ceremony and led the graduation ceremony without a hitch.

After completing PLDC, I was invited to attend a breakfast with the Sergeant Major of the Army. As an E4, I wanted to stand out from all the other people he came across. I decided that I needed to ask a question so that he would have to address me.

So that's what I did. It felt great. Whether he remembered me or not, I don't know, but my goal was accomplished.

The following year (and after a continuous stream of Airborne instructors, better known as Black Hats, trying to convince me to come to their company for Airborne School), one instructor invited me to view all the training to see what it was like. Though I wasn't planning on attending Airborne School, I figured it wouldn't hurt to see the training. He took me to Ground Branch where you learn proper the landing technique called a parachute landing fall or PLF. This training was conducted in a sawdust pit. That's all you did all day, over and over again: learn how to fall into a sawdust pit. By the end of the day, sawdust was everywhere: in your shoes, in your hair, inside your clothes.

Then he took me to Tower Branch and Jump Branch, where I actually went up in the aircraft with the students to watch them jump. I sat on the ramp inside the aircraft and watched them go out the door. It was great! One of the particular things I learned about jumping was that you couldn't look at the ground (which is unnatural). You tend to want to look where you're going, but that causes you to reach for the ground, and if you do that, you'll get injured.

In the end, because I could earn another $150 per month, I went through Airborne School and became jump-qualified. That was day-care money, which changed my perspective.

Airborne School was fun. In 1994, I went to Alpha Company, and my Airborne instructor was one of my basic training instructors! He didn't seem so scary this time. At Airborne School, there were about 400 students to a class (about a hundred per squad). Despite the fact that I worked at Battalion and all the Black Hats knew me, I somehow thought I could sit in the back in the corner and not be noticed. Not a chance. I was called out the very first day.

And once it became known among the other instructors that I was finally in training, I started to have a lot of visitors from my unit. During Airborne training, you had to do ten push-ups for each visitor that came to see you. So my visitors would say, "We're just checking on you to make sure you're doing okay. Now drop down and give me ten!" Once, I had about five Black Hats come to visit me the same day. That meant I had to do fifty push-ups—I didn't want any more visitors after that!

On the first day of training, all students were given a roster number that was displayed on the helmets we wore all day every day. They called all students by their roster number. Mine was 070 (zero seven zero), but they nicknamed me "Double Oh Seven."

During Tower Week (week two), we had to jump out of the thirty-four-foot tower, which simulated exiting an aircraft. At the top of the tower, we were hooked up to a zip line that, once we exited the pretend door, mimicked a parachute fall, minus the landing. I got to the door and was supposed to jump, but I had questions. I paused in the door, turned, and asked a question. The instructor answered my question, and I prepared to jump. But, then, I paused again and—same thing— he answered, and I prepared to jump. I did this a third time, and the instructor finally grabbed me and threw me out the door. I screamed all the way down, and then they changed my nickname from "Double Oh Seven" to "Screamer."

But eventually I passed and ended up being the Enlisted Honor Graduate out of 400 students in my class. That was a huge honor and meaningful affirmation that I was exceptional at anything I put my mind to. My basic training Drill Sergeant was the one who submitted my name for nomination. I was very proud of that.

After completing Airborne School, I took initiative and decided to compete for Soldier of the Month, which I won on my first go. After being promoted to Sgt./E-5 in 1995, I decided to do it again and, just as before, won NCO of the Month.

Unfair treatment

Since things had been going so well, I thought that the lie that had led to my "infraction" would be my only major bump in my journey. But it turns out that was just the beginning.

When Soldiers move from one duty station to another, they usually get what's called a PCS award, which is more like a parting gift. As I was moving from one duty station to the other, I noticed I wasn't getting these awards. In the military, you don't always get a pat on the back for everything you do. Sometimes, it's an oversight but other times, it's intentional. I brushed off this oversight because I was determined not to rely on other people's approval. I remember consciously deciding that, because I wasn't getting the "congratulations," the "good job," the ribbons, or the awards that everybody else was getting, I would decide for myself what success looked like.

Doing this was important to me. People will either help you succeed or try to control you so you don't outshine them, so I decided that I didn't need others approval. I did need to be successful—but I could define that. Since I had defined what was successful for me, the awards didn't matter. What really mattered was what I earned through hard work, such as Airborne, Pathfinder, maxing my PT test, my five foreign jump wings, and other tangible accomplishments that were not subject to interpretation. I didn't need the awards, the ribbons, the accolades. Those didn't matter. My evaluations that listed my achievements mattered, so I looked forward to those. If I met the qualifications for something and earned it, I wanted that recognition.

Now that I was an NCO, I would start receiving non-commissioned officer reports (NCOERs), the primary tool in the Evaluation Reporting System (ERS) used for documenting NCO performance and potential. The ERS identifies officers and NCOs who are best qualified for promotion and assignments to positions of higher responsibility. It also identifies Soldiers who should be kept on active duty, those who should be retained in grade, and those who should be eliminated. During my career, my accomplishments weren't always reflected on these reports. I used to assume that my accomplishments would magically appear on my evaluations, but I later learned that not all leaders operated that way. It was a common practice for the leader to ask their soldier for their accomplishments for that year so they could be annotated on their evaluations. So sometimes, it was understandable that my accomplishments wouldn't make it onto my evaluation report (NCOER) because I hadn't advocated for myself.

As time went on, I started fighting for the recognition that I had earned. That made me wonder what else I had to do in order to be treated fairly. Initially, I just took it. But later on, I had to fight to make sure I got credit on paper for the things I did. This was important because the higher you go, the more your records are looked at for different things like promotions, special assignments, and duties.

When a leader is looking to hire you for a certain position, they don't call you right away. They want to see your records to see what you look like on paper first. They want to see if you're worth their time and effort. If so, then you might be afforded new opportunities. There was no reason for those toxic leaders I had to treat me the way they did. There was no reason for them not to give me the credit I deserved.

The truth was they were only looking out for themselves. That was their "reason," if you could even call it that. When you first enter the military, you're groomed to see things from their perspective. You're groomed for "mission first." But after being in for a while, you realize that many of the people around you are not about "mission first." They are about themselves. The higher I got, the more I saw it. When the "mission first" that you swore an oath to comes in conflict with the selfish aims of those around you, you need to do something different. You need to assess the situation, recognize what you're dealing with, and act accordingly. The only way you can figure that out is if you ask yourself, "What does success look like, and how do I measure it?"

| 4 |

The Next Jump

After completing Airborne School in 1994, I decided it was time to leave the S-1 shop. Now that I had gone to PLDC and Airborne School (despite the Battalion secretary saying I never would), I requested and was moved to Jump Branch to be the supply Sergeant, which was another MOS I held. Once I got there, I wondered, "What else can I do to better myself?" I thought of Pathfinder School.

In order to attend, you had to fulfill one of the required MOSs and be at least an E4. Pathfinder School prepares Soldiers to become proficient in sling loads, helicopter landing zones and air assault planning, and drop zone operations. Around 1992 the 1/507th changed the MOS requirement to include supply MOSs. That same year, Staff Sgt. Hernandez, a female Black Hat, completed Pathfinder School. I looked up to her.

For an entire year, my Chain of Command gave me excuse after excuse for why I couldn't attend Pathfinder School. They said things like, "You know it's hard, and there's a lot of math." That didn't bother me because I was good at math. They were trying to make me take ownership of difficulties that were not mine. They also told me I needed to complete certain tasks before they would let me go. But whatever they asked for, I did. Finally, they said I could go if I passed the company run.

27

I was a good runner, but I could never keep up with the males. There was nothing that was going to make my legs move any faster, especially as short as I was. I decided to look at the official requirements to attend the course, and a company run wasn't on the list, so I threatened to file a complaint with the Inspector General (IG).

Once I did, I was given the opportunity to attend the course. What I learned is that people wanted so desperately to attend this school that some of them paid their own way. They would take leave from their units, come to Fort Benning, and stand in a formation on day one, waiting for a chance to take the place of someone who didn't show up. On day one, I had to stand in that formation, hoping for my name to be called. I still wasn't sure if I'd get in, but my name was called and I was in. They issued us field gear, but it wasn't mandatory. You just took what you thought you needed in case we needed to stay overnight in the field. I took a rucksack, sleeping bag, and a shelter half.

Back then, the school was only two weeks long. In my class of about thirty-two students, I was the only female, but I didn't think anything of it.

The first week went fine. The other male students and I got along, no problem. They were cordial. That is until I passed the inspection portion when they stopped speaking to me. Before starting the course, I had no idea that Pathfinder School had a 50% failure rate, and apparently, many failed the Inspection of Expedient Air Items and Inspection of Sling Loads.

To pass, you had to inspect sling load equipment and several objects, such as a crate or jeep that were rigged for sling loading, and find a certain number of deficiencies (gigs) in a given time limit. The gigs were installed on each item, and unlike Jumpmaster School, we weren't given a sequence. We could come up with our own. Mine was top to bottom, left to right. You not only have to know what the deficiencies look like but you also have to use the proper nomenclature.

When it was my turn to take the test, I was navigating the stations and noticed that I was missing one per station. You're only allowed to miss six altogether.

When I got to one station, the instructor (who knew me) told me, "You're not going to find these gigs." At first, I thought he was joking. But he wasn't. He said it again. "You're not going to find these." So, the challenge was on. Bet. I turned off the emotion and got to work. This was the first time I actually disconnected from stress in real time.

I went through my sequence from top to bottom and left to right. I called them out, found all of them, and moved on to the next station. I finished that week even though we lost half the class because the others failed.

Setting me up for failure

After I passed the first week and others didn't, well, from that point on, no one was cordial to me anymore. I don't know whether I was invading their territory since it was a "gentleman's course" or whether it was a personality conflict—theirs not mine—but in this instance, it wasn't just toxic leaders creating issues for me. My fellow Soldiers were as well. I didn't care. But I did care that they later set me up to fail.

For the second week, we had to go to the field and put all that training into practical application. We were given missions to fullfil (that was the leadership portion of the school). For each mission, you have a team leader and assistant team leader. Our job was to complete whatever mission was assigned to you, using the team that we had, and complete it within a certain amount of time. If we finished testing everyone that day, then we didn't have to stay out overnight.

We were going through the missions, and everybody was taking turns being in the leadership positions and testing out. As we were going from mission to mission, a five-ton truck would meet us at every site. It was the same truck, same driver. I was thinking that this was great because I reasoned there was no need for me to carry my personal gear on every mission. I could just leave it on the truck. Work smarter not harder, right?

For each mission, you only carried a piece of equipment assigned to you by the team leader in order to accomplish the mission. One of the lightest things was a tent peg and the heaviest thing was a PRC-77 radio.

We didn't finish that day, so we stayed overnight in the woods. I set up my shelter half and went to sleep next to a tree. When I got up the next morning, it was my turn to be the leader. I was hoping that I would not be the team leader. I was hoping that I would be the assistant. After all, it's all of these males and just me. I'm not trying to stick out. I'm just trying to make it.

But there was only one other E4 besides me in the class, and he wasn't Airborne-qualified. The rest were other sergeants and officers, so they made me team leader and some other male was my assistant. He was a mean-looking guy, but we had a mission to do. I just needed to be able to lead a team and set up a drop zone, helicopter landing zone, or pick-up zone within a time limit. While I'm going through my mission and getting stuff done, I noticed that all the males collectively decided to take their time. They were dragging feet.

Being the team leader, I was on the clock. I had to get my mission done, and these guys didn't seem to have the same sense of urgency as they did before. Suddenly, they didn't want to cooperate. But two of them decided to help.

"Come on. Let's get it done," they said. Between the three of us even, we still couldn't get it done on time. I failed. But I didn't just give in. I protested. I complained to the instructors. I told them, "You know what these guys did. You need to fix this." I told them that if they didn't,

I would go to the IG. They gave in and gave me another mission. This time, they cooperated like they were supposed to and I met my time.

Next, we had to take the written portion. For this test, we started out with one thousand points and deductions would be made from there. Since there were several formulas we had to memorize for the test, I used my scratch paper and wrote those down first. I took my time, but I always hated being the last one finished. I preferred to be the first. (I was almost always the first or second one to finish a test.)

We turned in our papers and waited for our test scores. Everyone knew we had to score at least 700 to pass, and anything over 700 was considered "extra work." It was understood that it was an honor to get a score of 700-something because then you became a member of the 700 Club. When I received my score, I was relieved and happy that I was a member. I was one of the guys.

When it came time for the group photo, none of the guys told me they were about to take it, and that's why I'm on the end by the door in our class photo. I decided to ask one of the students what happened when it was my turn to lead the mission. He told me I "wasn't pulling my own weight" because I decided to put my gear on the truck and I wasn't carrying my own gear. That was remarkable to me. Were they mad because they hadn't thought of it first? What did me carrying my personal gear have to do with accomplishing the mission? Absolutely nothing.

Derailing my path to success

After Pathfinder School, I looked for another challenge. Air Assault School was within my reach, so I went to the Training NCO and told him what I wanted. He told me that I couldn't go because I'd be "triple stacked." That meant that I would have had three badges on my uniform jacket instead of just two. Just having one was okay. Two was a pretty big deal. As a female, being both Airborne- and

Pathfinder-qualified was pretty major. But adding Air Assault was just too much for them to accept.

Instead of fighting for it, I decided I wanted to try my hand at Jumpmaster School; I wanted to get my Senior Wings. To earn the Senior Wings I had to have at least 30 static line jumps including 15 jumps with combat equipment, two night jumps with one as a Jumpmaster of a stick, (A stick, also called a chalk, is a load of paratroopers in one aircraft prepared for a drop), and two mass tactical jumps (an operation in which a battalion sized unit or larger moves personnel and equipment from one place to another by air). I also had to graduate from Jumpmaster School and serve on jump status for at least 24 months.. Since I worked at Jump Branch, I could pretty much jump when I wanted to. So I knew what I needed to do to qualify and began racking up a lot of jumps.

I got into Jumpmaster School and the instructors showed us the sequence called JMPI. JMPI (Jumpmaster Personnel Inspection) is the order in which every Jumpmaster inspects every jumper the exact same way every time. "You cannot negotiate the sequence," we were told. We also had to memorize the nomenclature and what's called "Pre-Jump," four pages of text that had to memorized by each Jumpmaster. This text is what's recited to all jumpers prior to boarding the aircraft for their jump. Again, I was the only female, but that was normal to me. Once we learned the sequence of how to inspect a jumper, we had to practice.

The class was divided in half, and we took turns between being the jumper and the "Jumpmaster." In order to pass the first week of training, we had to inspect three jumpers within five minutes and find all the gigs, using the proper nomenclature. So we formed a circle of jumpers and each "Jumpmaster" student went from jumper to jumper, going through the sequence.

If you were inspecting the jumpers, that was one thing. But if you had to wear the equipment (parachute, reserve parachute, rucksack, and weapons carrier), it got very tiring after a while. So we had to be in shape in order to carry all that gear and stand there and be inspected one "Jumpmaster" after the other until everyone had a turn. Then we had to switch out. Knowing your turn was coming, you wanted to make sure you stood up straight and just get through it.

All the students got to a point of getting through three jumpers within about four minutes and thirty seconds. The three jumpers were two "Hollywoods" (parachute and reserve) and one combat equipment jumper (parachute, reserve parachute, rucksack, and weapons carrier). The instructors told us to be careful when it came time to test, because we were going to go too slow and would run out of time. Every class did the same thing. When it came time for me to test (since I was getting through three jumpers in 4:30), I figured that I had time to make sure I caught all the gigs. Not so. I went way over five minutes.

Anyone who failed the first go-around was able to retest. I mentally made the corrections I needed. The test area was outside in back of the building. As soon as I turned the corner, I was in shock. My combat equipment jumper was well over six feet tall which was really tall, especially for someone like me! I'm five feet one. But I sucked it up. I've got this.

The instructor said, "Go." I got through the first two Hollywood jumpers without a hitch. "Put your hands on your head and tilt your head to the rear." I gave them the proper commands, "Turn!," "Hold!," "Squat!," "Recover!" Things were going smoothly until I got to the six foot tall final jumper, who was nonresponsive. I gave him commands, and he either wouldn't respond or would respond very slowly. I had to repeat myself, but I got through it. I tapped him on the back of his pack and yelled, "Have a good jump!" The clock was supposed to stop the moment I tapped the jumper. But after tapping him, I looked up at the instructor and saw he hadn't stopped it yet. I watched him stop the clock. It was like time was going in slow motion. I failed. I felt defeated. What could I do about it? I drove on.

I'm proud of this story because I put in the effort, and I succeeded in my eyes. It doesn't matter what they think. I did it for me. I was put through a lot in order to go to other schools and get promoted. They derailed my path to being triple stacked, and then they derailed my path to becoming a Jumpmaster. In the past, I had just kept my mouth shut and put up with the bullying. But I was done.

When I had first arrived at the 1/507th, I was bullied. The bullies were certain males in the unit who would call me names and crack jokes. Whether it was racism, sexism, or just outright toxic people, I would just take it at first. For a whole year, I took it. Finally, I got tired and started fighting back. I knew they wouldn't stop unless I did something about it, so I did. I threw it right back at them, and from that point forward, I started speaking up for myself.

I didn't get them back every time, but I did get in a few "gut punches," and they eventually left me alone.

For some reason, many in the military think their race or sex or another characteristic they may have affords them special treatment and a greater chance of success. And if you don't have those attributes, you don't deserve success. But you must understand that those attributes that others define for you aren't what determine your success or failure.

Finding my own path to success

If you're good at what you do and enjoy your job, then you have established a pattern that can't be easily denied. I happened to like the jobs I did. Being "the only one" was a habit and pattern throughout my military career. The choices I made were based on the person I was, and that defined the path I took. I was defiant. I was adamant. I knew my worth. When people would try to get to me, I would think to myself, "Is that all you've got? You're going to have to come a lot harder than this if you want to get me." I was confident: I knew I was intelligent, and I had faith in myself and my abilities. I knew that I had something to contribute. This is when I decided that, despite the conflict and hostility I was experiencing, I would create something fantastic/outstanding so that these people would have no choice but to remember me. They would have no choice because I did that. My name would be on the accomplishment, no one else's. A large part of my military legacy is that I was the "first" in a lot of things. I remember going to briefings where I was the only representative for my unit. Or I would be in a meeting and be the junior soldier in a room full of Sergeants Major and other officers. I remember consciously deciding that I was going to present myself confidently as if I belonged there. I had to exude confidence.

In some briefings, only important people sat at the table while everyone else sat along the wall behind them. Sometimes, I felt confident enough to grab a seat at the table, especially if I knew the material. As an E7 or E8, I was important and I owned that. Once I got there, I made sure I came up with a question or statement that I could contribute to the discussion to make sure the others looked at me and listened to my words.

My career highlights (found in the appendix at the end of this book), prove my success and were my "personal therapy." What many of my critics didn't understand was that my life's story hadn't been written yet, so I was trying to see what I could do. There was no one who could tell me I couldn't do or accomplish something and make me believe it. Once I set my mind to it, I took action. I didn't think twice. It was done.

Some people freeze in the presence of conflict. Some people would do anything to avoid confrontation. But freezing leads to paralysis and inaction because you stop thinking and processing information. I couldn't afford to do that. The situation doesn't go away when you freeze, so you have to deal with it in the best way possible. Instead, I disconnected from the trauma, reacting with facts and data instead of emotions, giving myself the best opportunity to get what I wanted.

There's a video I came across called Why It's CRITICAL To Detach in Real Time by Jocko Willink and Echo Charles. I was floored when I watched it because that's exactly what I was doing. I had no idea that was a "thing," and there it was being explained in perfect detail. When you detach from the trauma, you don't have to fear it. Once you get away from fear, you allow yourself to make rational decisions. Another approach I took is called acceptance. When I was going through all the trauma, hostility, and conflict, I decided to accept that that was the environment I was in. Once I did that, I was better able to manage what I was dealing with. Floyd Landis talks about this in an interview he did with Graham Bensinger called "Floyd Landis: Tour de France Is a War." Acceptance was huge. I remember being at work thinking, "This is who I'm dealing with. This is what I'm working with." Acceptance allowed me to act accordingly and freed me from my fear. The quicker I accepted, the quicker I could take action. I was strategic: fear is controlling, and I did not want to be controlled.

You might think that it's impossible or disingenuous to think this way, but it's not. Not if you make the decision to think and live this way. When you connect with your real self, you become an individual, and that's scary to some people. Even threatening. I wasn't trying to fit in, and I wasn't trying to get sympathy. I simply wanted to be helpful. I wanted to be outstanding and to mean something to my team, my Commanders, and my unit. I wanted to be remembered but in a good way. I wanted my best self to be equal to or better than others, especially the jokers around me.

| 5 |

Flight School

As I was working at Jump Branch, one by one, the people in my section were being sent to Korea. As an E4 at the time, I decided I didn't want to go, so I told people I wasn't going to Korea. Even with reassignment orders in hand, I was still adamant that I wasn't going, so I decided I would go to flight school.

Since I had always wanted to fly, I decided to submit my application. It took a year to get past it because of the physical alone. I was too short, my sitting height was too short, and my reach was too short. But because I was determined, I decided to request waivers for all of those requirements. I just needed the opportunity to show them that I could do it.

In order to be a pilot in the military, you had to either be a Commissioned Officer or a Warrant Officer, so I went to Warrant Officer Candidate School (WOCS) after Fort Benning. During WOCS, I left Eric with my sister, which ended up being a good move for me. But, when I got to flight school he said he missed me, so I made the decision to go get him and had him with me while I was in flight school. One of the added pressures of having a child on your own in the military is that you go from worrying about one person to worrying about two. I went from peanut butter and jelly sandwiches and ramen noodles to having to cook and worry about day care and elementary school. Having him with me when I was training made it even more difficult but not impossible. I just did what needed to be done.

Training was going along just fine until I noticed that the instructors were giving me "special" treatment. For some reason, they were giving me a hard time and I didn't understand why. Finally, I decided to confront those instructors and find out what the deal was. Just like Lieutenant Jordan O'Neil in GI Jane, I wanted to be treated the same as everyone else.

I asked the question and they gave me an answer. They told me that the reason I was treated differently was because they thought I could handle it because I was Airborne- and Pathfinder-qualified. In hindsight, I could have sterilized my uniform by removing my qualification badges before I arrived at the school, but then I would've been out of uniform. I told them that wasn't fair, and they agreed. I had no more issues after that.

After that, WOCS was a good experience for me. I learned to be even more detailed than I already was. One of the challenging aspects was that the students were all leaders in their own right. During the course we learned that we had far more leaders than followers, which presented a problem we didn't have time for. We had to be quick and proficient at everything, so it was difficult when it came to getting things done as a company. It was a lot of running (double-timing) everywhere with several people ordering you to drop down and do push-ups or leg lifts.

The exercises didn't bother me. I used them as an opportunity to improve my physical fitness. For my final PT test, I did sixty push-ups in a minute. The grader wanted me to keep going because I wasn't even tired. I did my two-mile run in 14:21, which was the best I'd ever done.

Every morning, the instructors would check our rooms to make sure everything was properly measured, aligned, and positioned. Your pillow, blanket, toothpaste, socks, T-shirts all had a specific arrangement. If anything was out of place, we were penalized by having to write a memorandum, in proper form, for each infraction. We had to describe what the infraction was, why it was wrong, and what we were going to do to fix it.

When we went to the dining facility, we couldn't just go in, get our food, sit down, and eat. We had to do what was called "dining rights." As we got our trays of food, we filled up one table at a time and the last one at the table had to lead the dining rights. I already memorized it just in case I got caught being the last one. And sure enough, I did— more than once—so I had plenty of practice leading dining rights.

You had to stay standing until the last person got to the table. The leader then says, "Take seats." Everyone sat in unison. Then came the commands:

"Ensure your tray is properly aligned to the edge of the table."

"Ensure your glass is properly positioned on the corner of your tray."

This proceeded until every aspect of your tray was checked for proper placement. Then we could eat.

Everyone had to have a spoon that was balanced right side up on the edge of your plate and the edge of your tray. Periodically, as you're eating, the spoon would fall off and you'd have to stop and replace the spoon before you could continue eating. This got annoying really quickly. We didn't have time to mess around with a stupid spoon.

Since we had to handwrite memoranda for everything, I decided to write one for the class, requesting permission to turn our spoons over. It worked. With that success, I wrote another memorandum requesting permission to graduate early so that no one would have to come back after the fourth of July holiday, including the instructors. It worked. They agreed. I was responsible for my entire class graduating early on July third.

My father, sister, and son were at my WOCS graduation ceremony, but I had an additional visitor, and I had no idea who this other person was. I hadn't invited anyone else. So I asked him how he knew about my graduation?" He turned out to be a member of the Black Aviators Association, and he said, "We knew you were coming."

When people find out that I was the only Warrant Officer who looked like me the entire time that I was there, they believe that it should have affected me. I never really thought about it. For me, I chose to see this as merely an observation and nothing else. I didn't dwell on what it might "mean" to others. That was their issue, not mine. I learned never to take ownership of things that weren't mine. When people ask me if it empowered me, I say that I was going to be my best self regardless.

After WOCS, I started flight school as a Warrant Officer. The first week was called Ground School, where we learned about airspace and weather. Then it was time to go to the aircraft. The first flight was called a "nickel ride" where we had to give the flight instructor a nickel with our birth year on it. Each aircraft had an instructor and two students. I flew first, so I was in the right front seat, which is where the pilot in command sits. The instructor took off, and the next thing I knew as we were in the air. The instructor said, "You have the controls." I looked at him like he was speaking Greek. He said it again, "You have the controls." I placed my hands on the cyclic and collective saying, "I have the controls." He responded with, "You have the controls," and then proceeded to remove his hands from the controls and place them on his lap. This is called a "three-way transfer of the controls." He placed them there because, peripherally, you'd always know when you were in control of the aircraft. All I did was fly in a straight line for what seemed like forever. I was afraid to deviate for fear of what would happen. This is how I learned what it meant to be in the "hot seat" because your brain is in overdrive when you have control of the aircraft. Before we got ready to land, I transferred the controls back to the instructor.

The first thing we had to do was learn how to hover. You had to be able to pick the aircraft up and hold it in the air without drifting. The class had a competition and the last one to learn how to do it would have to ride in circles on this bike that turned a big rotor on the top of it as you turned the pedals. I knew it was not going to be me.

When I tell people what it's like to hover, I ask them if they've ever balanced a broom upside down on their hand. I used to do this as a child all the time. In order to balance the broom, your hand has to be ever-so-slightly in constant motion. Hovering is the same concept. Your right hand is on the cyclic doing one thing, your left hand is doing something else, and your feet are on the foot pedals doing something else. All three things need to be in constant, ever-so-slight movement in order to keep the aircraft in the air in a constant position.

During my first few attempts, I lifted the aircraft up, but a moment later it veered off and the instructor regained the controls. I did this several times until I finally got it. Then the instructor told me to look to the right. I drifted to the right. After a while I got the hang of it, picked it up, looked right and held it steady. After a few seconds that seemed like an eternity I asked the instructor, "How long do I have to hold it, sir?" He replied, "Forever." It was a good experience.

During my next memorable experience, I had a new "stick buddy," a fellow flight student. I remembered him because he always had a problem trusting his instruments. He told me he flew fixed wing for a while and that explained why he was always out of trim. One day when we were on our way back from training, he was flying and I was in the back seat. As he was coming into to land, he was doing what felt like a nose dive to me . I thought, "Surely the instructor is going to say something." He took the controls, swung us around and let the student do another approach, which was a lot better. I'm so grateful for my stick buddy. Without him I would never have had a photo of me in the helicopter.

After IERW, Initial Entry Rotary Wing course, I started the next phase of training called Instruments. During this phase, we learned how to trust our instruments in order to fly the aircraft. In case you were caught in a white out or brown out, you had to rely on just your controls without using an outside reference. In order to train for this, we had to place a plastic strip over the visor on our helmets. We also had a curtain or panel that was put up over all windows so we couldn't see outside. When it was time to take off, the instructor would say, "Panel up, visor down." You would sit on the takeoff pad and wait for clearance. Then, once cleared for takeoff and using just your controls, you would take off to a certain altitude in a certain direction, fly around, and then return.

Two maneuvers I enjoyed doing were the autorotation and stuck pedal. These are emergency procedures that we practiced routinely. An autorotation is done in case of an engine failure. In order to simulate this, the instructor would reduce the engine to idle (which was not enough power to keep the aircraft in the air) and in turn, you were supposed to drop the collective (which controls elevation) in order to disconnect the rotor from the engine and start looking for a place to land. You could use the spinning momentum of the rotors to buy you enough time to land. If you've ever spun a hanger around on your finger and then it stopped spinning, this is the same concept. You would be flying around, and all of a sudden, the instructor would idle the engine and you were supposed to react. Sometimes the instructor would do it en route to a training, but he would recover the aircraft while we were still in the air. Other times when he did it, we actually had to land the aircraft.

Sometimes you could see his left hand slowly glide over to his side, and you knew it was coming.

A stuck pedal was simulated when the instructor would push one of the pedals all the way forward, which caused the nose of the aircraft to turn sideways. You can literally fly around sideways and find a place to land. As you got closer to the ground, you would slow your speed and reduce the engine power, which allows you to gradually straighten the aircraft as you came gliding to a complete stop.

After learning and perfecting all of these different maneuvers, I finally got to do my first solo. That was when two students would fly racetracks around the training airfield without the instructor. It was actually less hectic than flying with the instructor. My instructor got out of the aircraft, and my stick buddy climbed in the front left seat and took his place. Since I was so short, I had to use one of those big thick yellow car wash sponges resting on my leg so my hand could reach the controls of the cyclic. Just as if the instructor were there, I followed my checklists and took off. I did a racetrack around the airfield, then landed. I switched places with my stick buddy and he took his turn. Piece of cake!

While waiting for the next phase, Basic Combat Skills (BCS), all the students were given an assignment to occupy their time. I was assigned to organize an office that was full of books and magazines. They were everywhere, and I wasn't told how to organize them, so I created a library complete with its own numbering system.

Later on, I discovered that someone was looking for a short pilot. They were building this helicopter called the RAH-66 Comanche, and the cockpit was supposed to fit every pilot from the shortest to the tallest. They needed a short pilot to test with, and I had the fortunate opportunity to be that short pilot. I got to work with the team that designed the cockpit and was flown to Florida, and Connecticut to sit in mockups just to see if I could reach and touch different things within the cockpit.

All the student pilots who started BCS flew either the OH-58 or the UH-1h. Being short, I trained on the OH-58, and the taller student pilots trained on the UH-1h because it had adjustable seats and they could fly better in it. Flying the OH-58, which is similar to the TH-67, was challenging for me because the dashboard was higher than I could see over while sitting in the aircraft on the ground, and the seats were not adjustable. Once I took off, though, I could see just fine because of the forward attitude of the aircraft. Using the same logic for the taller student pilots with the adjustable seats, I wondered if I could also switch to the UH-1h. Just as I had requested to graduate early in WOCS, I requested to switch to the UH-1h, and after three days of flying the OH-58, my request was approved. Once I got in the UH-1h, I was amazed. I could see everything!

Everything was going quite well, but then one day I started having pains in my abdomen as I was at home preparing my maps for the next day. I brushed it aside and decided to take a break from the maps and put a relaxer in my hair. Just as I had finished adding this chemical to my hair, the pain grew a hundred times more intense in an instant. I keeled over. It was so painful. I had never felt anything like it. It was even worse than childbirth.

It was scary as well because something inside me was causing me this much pain, and I didn't know what it was. I called a friend who helped me wash the relaxer out of my hair and took me to the hospital. I felt every single bump in the road on the way there. I remember lying on the hospital bed and the doctor asked if I was pregnant.

"No. I'm in immense pain."

He gave me an ultrasound. I was still in pain. It was so intense. He gave me an IV and put something in it. I asked him when he was going to give me something for the pain, but he said he already had. I said it's not working. He gave me a second medication; still nothing. Finally, the third medicine he gave me worked. It turned out I had a ruptured ovarian cyst.

Once I healed, I was able to join another class and continue training.

| 6 |

Transition Pains

Though I fought for it, I ended up not finishing flight school.

I got involved with John who was my significant other for a short time, but he ended up not being a good person at all.

Relationship violence

It wasn't long before things got violent. We got into a massive argument one day. I lived in a townhouse, and I knew we were making a lot of noise. I remember slumping down on the floor between the bed and the closet and screaming my head off. I was trying to make as much noise as possible. As I was screaming, he swung his fist and punched me in the face. I guess he wanted to make me shut up, but I kept screaming. He picked me up and threw me on the bed and put his hands around my neck. I tried so very hard to push him off of me, but I couldn't do it. I wasn't strong enough. I remember thinking, "I'm not done," as I started to black out.

But then he released his grip, and I jumped up and ran into the bathroom and locked the door. He pleaded with me to open the door.

"NO!"

"You either open the door, or I'm going to take the doorknob off," he threatened. Then it got quiet. He went and got a screwdriver and proceeded to slowly unscrew each screw, take the doorknob off, and enter the bathroom. I was crying and he thought he could make up for what he had just done to me a few minutes before by trying to hold me. I wasn't having any of that. I fought him again. In trying to get him off of me, he gave up, and threw me down on the floor. I banged my head on the side of the tub on the way down. Then he left.

I had my first black eye. Despite this, he somehow convinced me to go to Eric's T-ball game. And just like the domestic violence in the movies and the news stories you hear about on TV, I was embarrassed by my injury, not by the fact that he caused it. I wore oversized sunglasses to hide the shame. When I went to training, I remember one of the students asking me why I had scratches on my neck. I made up an excuse instead of telling him the truth.

It was a nightmare that just kept getting worse. John threatened me with horrible things that sounded preposterous, but they ended up happening. He told me, "I'm going to take your things and sell them to the pawn shop, and you're going to have to buy them back. That's the only way you're going to get your things back. I'm even going to have you arrested and you're going to go to jail, and I won't even have to show up to court." One day, I came home from training and my house was a mess. Stuff was everywhere. He had put all of my clothes in garbage bags, but what I really noticed was that he had taken my flight gear, uniforms, civilian clothes, underwear, Bose speakers, and even my clarinet. I remembered that he had told me he would do this—and he did. I know that he must have had people helping him because he didn't have a vehicle or his own money.

What I later learned was that he had faked being a member of a fraternity. He even went so far as to have their emblem tattooed on his arm. He figured out their secrets and used this knowledge to fool them into supporting him. One of these so-called friends of his had my clothes, uniforms, and flight gear. I went to his house and retrieved them from his wife. I later found a pawn slip, so I knew where I could buy back my speakers and clarinet.

Despite everything he had done to me, he successfully convinced me that if I married him, things would be different, so after three months, we did. He almost convinced me to buy a house with him. I never thought this would be me—someone who stayed in an abusive relationship—but I learned why women stay.

Women stay in bad relationships for various reasons. For me, I stayed as long as I did because I kept believing him when he said he didn't mean it. One afternoon, we went to the pool even though I couldn't swim. He took me to the deep end and let me go. As I went under the water, he grabbed me and pulled me up and laughed. That should've been a warning to me, but he said he was sorry. Then he started saying he would do things that made absolutely no sense, including taking my vehicle. He even claimed he could have me kicked out of flight school and out of the Army. He was just a civilian with no job. How was he supposed to manage all that? Things were getting progressively worse, but I still stayed.

One day while I was at work, in between phases of training, he called me and said he had my vehicle. How was that possible? He couldn't get on the base without an ID, which he didn't have. He couldn't drive himself because he didn't have his own vehicle. He had no money but he did have my spare key. He told me to look outside. Sure enough, my vehicle was gone. "Don't worry," he said. I'll come pick you up.

It took me three months of being fooled and then another three months to finally escape. Since I couldn't get him to leave or to stop abusing me, I decided to take Eric and go to a women's shelter in Dothan. We stayed there for three days, but then I went back to him. I went back because the shelter was not the answer. It was temporary and I needed a permanent solution.

The final straw was when he threatened that he would take Eric away and that I would never see him again. That snapped me out of it. Within three weeks of being married, I was able to get an annulment. I asked so many people for help dealing with him, and I just wasn't getting any. I asked my Chain of Command; I even asked the Black Aviators Association for help. Nothing.

I eventually got attorneys involved, but the first one was totally useless. She didn't speak up for me and ended up being a crook. If you've ever seen the movie, Enough with Jennifer Lopez, this is what I was dealing with. In order to focus on the battle at hand, I decided to take Eric to my sister's and come back to fight. The attorney stood in front of the judge and said nothing to defend me. The judge ended up forcing me to go get my son and turn him over to John, no proof of paternity required, no proof that he had a means to take care of my son—and I had two days to do it. I couldn't believe it. I kept waiting for my attorney to say something but she never spoke up for me. She didn't protest this decision or demand anything on my behalf. Another one of his prophecies came true. So I fired her and got a better attorney who was a great advocate.

It took me about three weeks, but I eventually got my son back. One day, I asked him, "Eric, where were you?" Since I knew John didn't have a job, money, or vehicle, I wanted to know how he took care of my son and where he kept him. My son said that he was at this lady's house. I somehow thought that if I drove him around town, we could figure out where he was for the time he was away from me.

I asked him, "Is it this way? Is it that way?" Believe it or not, we found the house where he had been staying. I knew that my son was so smart. We went to the door, and sure enough the woman knew Eric. She said that some guy had dropped him off and just left him there. He didn't give her any money or anything to take care of him. But she took it upon herself to buy things for him. She bought him a sleeping mat for school, bought his lunches, and made sure he was fed. She took care of my son.

I thought getting Eric back and getting an annulment would be the end of the nightmare with John but my fight was still not over. Because he kept saying he would do things and they would come true, I decided that I needed to make sure my son was taken care of.

One day, he came over but by then I had changed the locks. He begged me to open the door, but I wouldn't do it. He said that if I didn't open the door, he was going to have me arrested. ME, arrested? I hadn't done anything. What he did was file a bench warrant accusing me of assault that he could call in at any time, and that's what he did. The police came and I had to go to jail. I didn't have to wear handcuffs and I didn't have to ride in the police car though. It's a good thing my dad was visiting me from New Orleans at the time because the officer let me ride with my dad to the jail, where I was booked for assault. John had an old, already healed scar on his forehead that he told the police that I did to him. My dad paid my bail, and sure enough, I went to court and he wasn't even there. Another one of his prophecies came true. Luckily, I told the judge that I had come there with no record and that I'd like to leave that way. The charges were dismissed, and my record was expunged.

Yet somehow, my ex again gained access to my townhouse. I called him and he was there with my son who was in his room asleep. I was going to confront him one last time. I went to the base hotel and got a room. I used the scratch paper in the room and wrote out a will and left it in the room, dictating that my sister was to have all my possessions and custody of my son. I went to a local store and bought some sleeping capsules and a purple drink. I took a bunch of the capsules apart and emptied them into the drink and headed home. When I got there, John was in the living room watching TV. I went to the kitchen and drank as much of the drink that I could and tossed the bottle in the garbage. My son was still upstairs asleep. I wasn't afraid that he would be injured. I only feared for myself. Then we laid together on the sofa and I waited because I knew what I had done.

As we were laying there, he was rubbing my arm and then next thing I knew I was on the floor. I couldn't move my limbs. I was paralyzed. But I was very much aware. I heard him say, "Erinn, what's wrong"? I could hear the panic in his voice. "Oh, my God, what did you do?" He was terrified. He ran to the kitchen and saw the bottle in the garbage. "What did you take?" As I was lying there, hearing the panic in his voice, I was so at peace. It was an indescribable calmness that I felt because I had finally won. I got what I wanted—and that was out of the relationship once and for all—and I needed to make sure my son was cared for. He couldn't hurt me or my son anymore. The fight was over. I didn't have to worry any more. I felt at peace for the first time in a long time.

Most times when someone attempts to end their life, it's because they've given up. They have no reason to live anymore. They may feel useless, abandoned, hopeless, and even helpless. But I was never any of those things. In that moment, I felt defiant and victorious. What I had accomplished was a solution to a problem. Nothing more. The ambulance arrived, and I went to the hospital, blacking out along the way. The next moment, I remember that I was lying on a hospital bed with a tube stuck up my nose and down my throat. My stomach was being pumped. I believe there was charcoal involved. I woke up thinking that I must've made the wrong decision and was being given another chance to get it right. A funny thing happened while I was there. My Commander and First Sergeant showed up, asking how they could help me. These were useless people.

Leaving the military

I was eventually released from the hospital and was able to recycle into another class. But it wasn't meant to be. I couldn't get it done.

After being given several chances, I failed an important check-ride and wasn't able to finish the course. Even though I had managed to accumulate over 120 flight hours, I felt like a failure because I had it all planned out. I wanted to fly Chinooks because it was the biggest thing out there at the time.

Because I couldn't finish flight school, as a Warrant Officer, I tried switching my MOS to Human Resources. I actually drove straight from Fort Rucker, Alabama, to Arlington, Virginia, to apply for this MOS change, but it didn't work out. I think I was denied because I didn't have enough college. I was so disappointed that I turned around and came straight back. I didn't even stay overnight. I had the option of going back to my previous unit, not as a Warrant Officer, but as a Sgt./E5. This was the rank I held prior to WOCS. To me, that meant going back as a failure so I elected to get out of the military.

By the time I left the military, Eric was in the second or third grade. Most military kids experience going to several different schools, but Eric didn't have that experience. Thanks to the decisions I made over the next couple of years, I was able to provide him more stability.

When I got out of the military, I lost about $20,000 annually, and I needed to make that up. So, I moved to Nashville where Erica lived. During that first year alone, I had six jobs at one time and was trying to fit in another one. I had four part-time waitress jobs, and one full-time job (I started off as a secretary, then a car salesman, then a support technician for Dell), and I was in the National Guard as a "Weekend Warrior." I took no breaks. Even though Erica was there, I had to take care of things myself. It was my responsibility. I put my son in daycare and nighttime care when I worked at night. It was extremely difficult. But like I've said, I just made the decision and dealt with it.

Even though I was missing the financial support of the military, I still maintained that going back to my old unit would have been a bigger failure than getting out. The pain of seeing them watch me not complete something I set out to do was worse than all of the pressure I found myself under outside the military.

But here is what I learned about putting all of that pressure on yourself that isn't yours to bear: other people aren't even thinking about you. The people you're performing for aren't thinking about you every waking moment of their day. They have their own lives to live. You don't take up as much space in other people's minds as you think. I wish I understood that a long time ago. But when I was going through it, I wasn't thinking that way.

For one entire year, I had some job to report to every day of the week. A couple of the jobs were actually fun. I waitressed at a sports bar and several nightclubs around town. It seemed like I was just working to pay for childcare, though. There was almost nothing left over.

Something had to give. That's when I started teaching my son that he had to learn how to stay at home by himself. It took a lot of work, but it worked out very well once I taught him that things were going to be okay and that nothing was going to happen to him if he followed my directions. I think that laying that groundwork early on helped him as he got older. Though parenthood isn't easy, there's light at the end of the tunnel. During the journey, you need to take it one decision at a time. A day at a time can be too long. One decision at a time.

Be willing to ask for help

I don't recommend it, but I did all of this with no support system. I never capitalized on the fact that I was a veteran. It hadn't dawned on me to even bring it up. Once I left the military, that part of my life was over, and I had moved on to the next thing. In fact, this never crosses the minds of a lot of veterans. We should be taken care of, especially after service to our country, but I had no idea that there were resources out there to help me.

This was the year that I learned an important lesson: I didn't have to do everything on my own.

In 1999, the Dell plant opened in Nashville, and they were hiring. Even though I had a full-time job and the part-time waitressing jobs at the time, I needed a full-time job that paid more . I decided to apply for their support technician job. To be a support technician, you have to learn how to install a computer operating system.

I had no idea how to do that. But after applying, they gave us a week of training. In order to get hired, they gave each of us a blank hard drive, software, and tools. We had to make the computer function. That was the test. I did it, and I got hired.

I was ecstatic because I had been having such a hard time making ends meet. My sister had just convinced me to apply for food stamps. I didn't want to because that was a handout, and I felt way too proud to accept it, but I went to the local food stamp office, took a number, and waited my turn. When my number was called, I cried all the way to the counter. Each step was heavier than the last. The clerk asked me if I had a job and I told her I just got a job at Dell. She, at first, disapproved my application because of this, but I pleaded with her because I wasn't going to receive my first paycheck for another two weeks. I never once mentioned that I was a military veteran. Thankfully, she changed her mind.

On my way out the door, a man stopped me and offered to help me. I didn't know why and I didn't know who he was, but I accepted. I was desperate enough to take it. I had only made $200 that month and was about to be evicted, so he gave me enough to cover my rent. He made me promise to pay him back and I did, every penny.

I was on food stamps for three months, which is what I was approved for. At the end of the three months I thought my benefits were over when they asked me if I still had a job. Since I was still working, as a reward, they gave me an extra three months of benefits. That assured me that I was doing the right thing and that they were rewarding me because of it.

My goal at Dell was to last at least a year, and then I would find something else because it didn't fulfill me and was stressful. They kept statistics on everything you did, like how many calls you took that day, how long you were on each call, how many times the customer called back, if they called back for the same issue, whether you had to send a part or a technician, how many times you had to send a part or technician, etc. I wound up being there for one year and four months.

Going back

When 9–11 happened and I watched the news showing the planes crashing into the towers, I decided that I wanted to go back into the military full time because I wanted to serve my country. I decided to quit my job at Dell and apply for a job with the Tennessee National Guard. I out-processed from the company and, as an ex-employee, I was escorted out of the building, which was standard procedure. As I was leaving, my colleagues told me they were proud of me for my decision and I appreciated that.

| 7 |

Second Wind

I was already in the Tennessee National Guard and in order to get a full-time job, all I had to do was to put my name in the hat. But first, they needed to get to know me, which meant I had to start applying for jobs. At first, I received two or three part-time orders that lasted anywhere from thirty to sixty days each. I kept applying so that the Tennessee National Guard would be familiar with me and see me as an asset. I finally applied for an Active Guard/Reserve (AGR) job on the 45th Civil Support Team (Weapons of Mass Destruction). AGR is a program where National Guard soldiers serve full time and enjoy the same benefits of active duty soldiers.

People ask me why I went back into the military full time after making the decision to leave. The military is what I knew. It was familiarity. It was structure, and it was certainty. I ended up staying in the National Guard on active duty for the remainder of my military career.

By the time I joined the National Guard full time, my son was nine. Because I was so busy trying to take care of us, I never asked him how my going back into the military affected him. It didn't occur to me at the time to speak to my son about these things. I saw things that needed to be done, and I took action. I made decisions and didn't hesitate. He was such a good kid and didn't require a lot from me.

A new opportunity

I was one of the two females in my unit, but then the other female quit. There were others who came and went. One of my colleagues later told me, "You know what, even though other guys came and went, you were the one that stayed." I think they told me that because they knew I would never let them down. I was glad they hired me. I knew I would do well and I liked my job. It did cross my mind, though, that I may have been hired to fill a quota. I was a "two in one." (female and Black). The Commander even confirmed this. But I consciously decided that I was going to do my best regardless. There was no pre-conceived notion that would fit me because I was very good at my job. I was a professional. I would give them no excuses to treat me as "less than" or "other than." This was an opportunity, and I was going to take full advantage of it.

And this time around I would ignore the bullies. Some people were always going to be toxic individuals. But I had news for them. They were going to see me. They were going to hear me. And I was going to make sure that when I left, they were going to remember me. I was going to leave my mark. I never needed to force anyone to accept me because I decided that my actions and my work would speak for me. There would be no excuse not to treat me with respect because I would demand it by my presence. As a result, I was well-respected among peers, subordinates, and superiors.

The guys I worked with used to talk about their wives or significant others, saying how they were such a nag among other things. I knew I didn't want to be that person, so I listened and learned what not to do. Not only was I a true professional, but I also worked well with others, especially in the all-male environments I found myself in. Why would I choose such a thing? I think it's not only because those were the jobs I enjoyed and was very successful at but also because I was in control of my own destiny. It was my choice.

Because that job was original, I ended up playing a unique role. As the Admin NCO and Decontamination NCO, it was my responsibility to develop methods and operating procedures to incorporate into the team's mission, which dealt with detecting weapons of mass destruction. Each team member had that same responsibility. And since the unit was so small (only twenty-two members, both Air and Army Guard), it was crucial that we each did our part.

Our goal as a new unit was to become federally certified to perform the function of a Civil Support Team. This involved a massive amount of training. Not only classroom and online training but also training missions once a month. Every month, we went out as a team and honed our skills in preparation for the final test, which was called an exit evaluation (EXEVAL). Later on, I was promoted to SSG/E6 and became the Training NCO and Assistant Operations NCO. By this time, I had a male Air Guard NCO working for me as my Admin/ Decon NCO.

As the Assistant Operations NCO, I was responsible for coordinating all of our travel— making all travel arrangements, creating all travel orders, and securing lodging, space to park our vehicles at the hotels, and places to eat when we got to our destination. I made sure we were taken care of. Because it was the guys and just me, I decided that my criteria for selecting lodging for us was walking distance to eateries (preferably near a Hooters, their favorite) and near a shopping mall for me. That was it. Anytime we went out to eat, the guys took care of me. They always looked out for me. They were like brothers I never had.

Hostility from the Commander

As it got closer to D-Day, the Commander got this bright idea that he wanted us to wear uniforms as we transitioned from the hot zone to the cold zone. The hot zone was the area of operation that contained the "hazard." His intent was that "We train as we fight." My position during the mission was on the Decon line in the warm zone where I scrubbed down each team member who exited the hot zone on their way to the cold zone. As the guys went from the hot zone and through my Decon line to the final shower, the Commander thought we should exit the shower wearing just a bath towel to get to the cold zone. I was not going to do that. The shower was approximately 5 ft. by 5 ft. square with an entry and exit door that were translucent. Up to that point, we had been wearing our fitness uniform during our training exercises. So when we went through the shower, we were still clothed. I absolutely refused. During the meeting, I told him directly, "Sir, I'm not doing that." He replied, "What's the matter Sgt. Watkins? We all sleep together."

One day, we were out on another training mission and my Airman and I were both sitting in the back of our trailer in our full gear (SCBAs, PPE, with radios) waiting for the guys (the survey team) to come back from the hot zone with a sample of the "contaminant." While we were sitting there, I had a heart-to-heart talk with him. He was very respectful and very conservative. I told him that I wasn't going to make him do something I wouldn't do, and he didn't have to wear just a bath towel if he didn't want to. It turns out that my hand was on my mic and the Medical Officer said, "Sgt. Watkins, your mic is on." They all heard every word I said. But for me, nothing changed. I meant what I said.

The day of our EXEVAL, a lot of media, public officials, and other observers were there. I was so angry because I knew what the Commander wanted me to do and I knew what I wasn't going to do. During missions, our Physician's Assistant regularly checked our blood pressure. That day, mine was 200/100. I had never known it to be that high before. But though I was angry, I felt calm. We got through the day without a hitch. I didn't wear the towel and my Airman didn't either. We both wore our fitness uniforms. Neither one of us got in trouble and nothing was mentioned about it again.

After that, I knew I had to get out of there. There was a lot of conflict and hostility coming from my Commander when I just wanted him to leave me alone so I could do my work. I didn't have time for his foolishness. I had a job to do. My colleagues depended on me, and I wasn't about to let them down.

So I found another job on another new Civil Support Team in New Jersey. If I was hired, this job would mean a promotion for me. In the National Guard, you can't be afraid to move if you want to progress and get promoted. I interviewed over the phone and got the job. I just needed to tell my Commander. Good thing he was out of town at the time because the Deputy Commander approved my reassignment and signed my clearing papers. By the time my Commander returned, I was already clearing.

He must've been fuming that I was leaving him, but if it hadn't been for him, I would've stayed. After I had my assignment and before I left, I heard him talking on the phone. My desk was positioned right outside of his office. I didn't make a habit of listening to his conversations but something caught my attention.

"You know she's a single parent and she has a son."

He was actually on the phone with my incoming Commander, trying to sabotage me before I got there. Because of this, I decided to leave Eric with my sister (which would give him more stability) and move to New Jersey by myself as a geographical bachelor, living on base just minutes from the unit. There would be no excuses why I couldn't do my job. My sister took my son, and he never missed a beat. He didn't need to change schools, and he caught the same bus home.

Praise from leadership

I went to my second leadership school, BNCOC "bee-nock" (Basic Non-Commissioned Officer Course). I went to Phase 1 in June and

Phase 2 in December of 2003, and I did very well. I was the Distinguished Honor Graduate both times.

One afternoon in June 2004, the Operations Officer, CPT Lee Sharber, said he needed to counsel me. I thought, "Oh no, what now?" As he read it, I started smiling.

"SSG Watkins will strive to maintain the standards that she has shown she is capable of in the training area. SSG Watkins understand the importance of prior coordination with section leaders to ensure the training schedules are accurate and produced in a timely manner. SSG Watkins will continue to keep her superiors abreast of any training issues that can only be resolved at a higher level.

. . . SSG Watkins will continue to be a "team player," displaying her "can-do" attitude in all that she does. SSG Watkins has shown, during the month of May 2004, that she is capable of performing at a higher level. Her organizational skills and military bearing have taken a dramatic improvement over the previous months. Her job performance has been noticed by all team members, not just those that she interacts with on a daily basis."

It was actually a counseling statement encouraging me to continue being the good Soldier that I was. It was totally unexpected, and I was very happy. It lifted my spirits and I greatly appreciated it.

Fighting through the fear and anger

I transferred to the 21st Civil Support Team in New Jersey as their new Operations NCO and Modeler. This transfer also came with a promotion to SFC/E7. As the Modeler, my job included using GIS, geographic information system software, current weather conditions at the incident location, and preloaded data about the suspected "contaminant" to plot hazard plumes used by the Commander to manage an incident. Using the models I created, the Commander was able to determine the best direction of approach so we wouldn't drive into a hazard as it traveled from the point of origin. I usually made several models before we left and would update this en route to the incident location. In order to do this, I had to able to connect my laptop in the command vehicle to the satellite dish on the roof of the vehicle so I could use the internet en route to a mission. Since I had designed websites as a hobby when I worked at Dell, I decided to create a local website for myself that included all the links to websites and documents that I would need for every mission. I called it my "Get Out the Door" website.

Once more, I got along well with my colleagues on the Civil Support Team but was having conflict with leadership. I had a lot to offer this new team, especially coming from a team that had already been federally certified. I was a valuable asset with a wealth of knowledge and experience.

I already knew the environment well and got along great with the guys just as I had when I was with the 45th CST. But then things started getting weird. It felt like I was being set up for failure by my leadership. I was receiving harsh treatment from them for things that were out of my control. It didn't make any sense to me.

By this time, I was extremely angry. My anger was internal so I hid it well, but I stopped caring because I was disgusted and tired of fighting. I had had enough. But little did I know I still had some fight left in me. I had the will to survive. I started looking for sources of inspiration that could help me deal with what I was going through. Though I was angry, the anger came from fear. People try to control you with fear, and I did not like being controlled. I wanted my actions to be my own. I wanted my decisions to be my own. So I looked online for something to help me deal with fear.

I came across this prayer by St. Francis de Sales called "Be at Peace":

Do not fear what may happen tomorrow;

the same understanding Father who cares for

you today will take care of you then and every day.

He will either shield you from suffering

or will give you unfailing strength to bear it.

Be at peace,

and put aside all anxious thoughts and imaginations.

Even though I wasn't religious, the significance of this poem cannot be understated. I was always afraid, and I was tired of it. I decided that I could take anything and use it to suit my own purposes, so this prayer was very helpful to me. What it meant to me was that I already possessed everything I needed to handle whatever came my way. Either adversity wouldn't affect me or I would be strong enough to bear it. So there was no need to worry any more. This prayer resonated with me so much that I printed it out and posted it right above my desk so I could look up and see it every day and throughout the day.

The next thing I did to combat my anger was look for something fun to do. I found a grown-up party in Philly. You had to be twenty-five and older to attend, and it was fancy so you had to dress up. Since it was December, people were wearing furs, long gowns, dress suits, and a few tuxes. Some of the suits were very colorful.

There were several different rooms of entertainment: oldies, new school, a live band, salsa, comedy, and a soul line dance room. Since I knew how to do the Electric Slide I decided to check out the line dance room. It was far beyond my expectations. The steps were intricate and complicated. How did they know all the steps? Someone told me, "You gotta go to class." So that's what I did.

I went online and searched for all the soul line dance classes I could fit into a week. I was going all over New Jersey, Philly, and even Delaware just to learn as many dances as I could. Then I went to the soul line dance parties on the weekend and stayed on the floor. I discovered that soul line dancing was such good exercise that I shaved two whole minutes off my two-mile PT run.

As I started going to these soul line dance events on the weekend, sometimes the DJ would play an oldies song. The first time I heard one, I didn't know what to make of it. It was before my time so I ignored it, that is, until I noticed younger people were getting up to dance to it. But what was this new dance style I had never seen before? I wanted to learn it because it looked like a lot of fun. This eventually led to my mastering the Philly bop, swing dance, two step, and strand. These styles were easy to pick up because I already knew how to salsa. Back in the day when my sister and I were little girls, our mother used to teach the hustle, and she would use us as demonstrators.

With my fear in check and my social life in a better spot, I was back on track.

Life kept trying to push me down

Life was going well, but then even stranger things started to occur. I noticed that someone was stealing my gear. All team members kept their gear in the same storage area so it would be ready when we were called for a mission. Except mine ended up missing. Sometimes it would turn up again or I was able to replace it.

When we went on training missions, I always rode in the command vehicle which had a satellite on the roof. The Commander and Ops Officer rode in the front seat, and the First Sergeant sat in the back seat with me. When I got in the vehicle, I had one little adapter that I kept in the same place every time: in the back pocket of the front passenger seat, so I could connect my laptop to the satellite and use the internet en route. During one mission, I got in the vehicle and reached for the adapter. It wasn't there. But I didn't miss a beat. I said nothing but used my cell phone to call "reach back" (NGB) and ask for the information I needed.

"What's the weather at our destination?" The guy on the other line replied, "Which one do you want? The airport? The news station?"

I was fuming, "Just give me the G**d*** weather!" He answered my question promptly.

As soon as we got to our location and the communications NCO set up his satellite dish, I was home free. I set up my Decon line with my assistant, and the rest of the day went off without a hitch. We got back to the unit, and I decided that I was going to tear the vehicle apart to find that adapter. As soon as I got out, the First Sergeant said, "You want me to help you find it?"

I told her, "No thank you. I'll find it." And she left.

I looked on my side first, then I went to her side. I found it. It was right under her seat. When people did things like this to me, I called them all kinds of names... in my head: "You big dummy. You idiot. You wuss!"

Later on, we went on a mission to Atlantic City, where we had our same simulated "recall" phone call. But since we were all staying in the same hotel on the same floor, I just went downstairs and met them in the parking lot. I got there before some of them did, so I felt that I was on time.

The Commander came up to me, yelling at the top of his lungs in front of the other team members. Imagine a big gorilla wearing a tutu barking at you . That's what I felt. He didn't scare me at all. He was asking me why I hadn't responded to the text message. But I was thinking, "I'm here so why do I need to respond?" I then took out my phone and sent him a text message on the spot.

"There. You're notified." That was so not smart. It was certainly self-sabotage.

When we got back to the unit, he called me into his office for what happened in Atlantic City. It was the Commander, Deputy Commander, Operations Officer, First Sergeant, and me. He began chastising me and said, "You're a poor excuse for a Soldier."

I immediately smiled because I knew that that wasn't true. I guess he saw that he wasn't getting to me, so he kicked me out of the office. The next thing I knew, he gave me a Letter of Reprimand (LOR) stating, "While I was counseling you, a wide grin and delighted, sarcastic look appeared upon your face. I immediately ordered you out of my office." I win again! I won because, in that moment, I controlled the dynamics of the conversation. His intent was probably to make me feel less than an outstanding Soldier, but I refused to let that happen. Mentally, I was in a good place and it showed. I knew who I was and he couldn't make me believe any different.

After that, I received a recommendation for involuntary separation. This meant that I was going to be fired from the National Guard. I was going to lose my job in a state where I had no family. This recommendation came in the form of a DA Form 4187. On this form at paragraph 2, it states that the involuntary separation recommendation goes through the intermediate Commander(s) to the Separation Authority. Since this was only a recommendation from the Commander, I knew I needed to get to the Approving Authority. Since this person, the Adjutant General of the State of New Jersey (TAG), had the power to end my career, I needed him to know who I was. I needed him to see me and understand the caliber of Soldier that was being recommended for separation.

I wrote up a rebuttal the size of an encyclopedia, made five copies, and went to the Legal Aid office on base. I had talked to him before about my situation, so he knew me.

When I walked into his office, I said, "Here you go, sir. I received a recommendation for involuntary separation and wrote a rebuttal. This is your copy. I'm going to see the General." I turned to walk away. He didn't let me make two steps toward the door when he replied, "Wait a minute, Sergeant Watkins. Let me make a few phone calls."

I was on a mission to see the General, the Approving Authority, and I felt it was Legal Aid's job to make sure I didn't get there. Because he stopped me from leaving, that let me know that he did not want me to get to the General, which is what he's supposed to do. I did not think that some General wanted to hear about some Sergeant First Class having personality issues in her unit. There were certainly more pressing issues to be concerned about. I also did not think that my Chain of Command wanted me to plead my case to some General about personality issues in their unit. Turns out, I was right.

In situations like this, the Soldier is usually transferred to another unit to see if that solves the problem. I was transferred to Joint Force Headquarters in Lawrenceville, New Jersey.

I called the Equal Opportunity Sergeant Major at NGB for help finding a way out of my current situation. I needed advice because I still didn't know what was going to happen to me. Even though I was assigned to JFHQ, I felt the assignment was only temporary and I needed a more permanent solution. He was very helpful. Of all that he told me, what I remember was his question, "Who is on your team?"

I asked him, "What are you talking about?"

He responded, "Well, who is on your team? Who is helping you?"

I internalized what he meant as anyone who is not against me is on my team. So some of my colleagues may not have known it, but they were on my team. If you just did your job, you were on my team.

I can put you on the field, or I can make you sit on the bench. I can kick you off my team if I want, and I can also add you back to my team if I want. If I decide that you've done something so bad that I want to get rid of you, then you're done. I'm crossing you off the list. You're off the team, no matter who you are. But if at some point in time you come back into my good graces, I can let you sit on the bench or put you on the field. All of this depends on what you're doing for me. Are you helping me or hurting me? After that conversation, I realized I wasn't as alone as I thought. I went back to work and noticed all the people who were helping me, including the people who were helping by just doing their job. I put all of these people on my team.

After being transferred to JFHQ, I had to attend my next leadership school, which was called ANCOC "ay-nock" (Advanced Non-Commissioned Officer Course) at Fort Jackson, South Carolina. In order to attend this school, you couldn't have any "flags" and you couldn't be on a profile. A flag is a document used by Commanders to bar Soldiers from receiving favorable actions such as schools and awards. Being on a profile meant that you had a physical defect that prevented you from demonstrating your physical readiness. Neither of these applied to me because the Commander would've counseled me if I had a flag and he would not have approved for me to go to the school in the first place. I also had just taken an APFT, Army Physical Fitness Test, the previous month and passed it with flying colors.

One day, I checked my medical file online and noticed that it indicated I was on profile, but I wasn't. I wasn't injured in any way. Using a copy of the APFT that I had just taken, I was able to have this corrected.

In this new unit, part of my job required me to frequently visit the office where personnel actions are processed, so they knew me quite well. One day, I went there and a woman who worked there called me over because she wanted to show me something. I went behind the counter and there was a box of documents that she was processing at her feet. She pulled one out and showed it to me. To my astonishment, it was a "flag" with my name on it. How can that be? I was never counseled about it. I had no idea how it got there. Who submitted it? I looked at the bottom and it was definitely signed by my previous Commander. Only it hadn't been processed yet. I knew this because every document that's processed is dated and time stamped, and this document didn't have either. She gave me a copy and I went on my way.

I drove down to Fort Jackson, South Carolina, for ANCOC. On day one, while the instructor was taking attendance, I was called out of the classroom. I had to report to the First Sergeant. I went to her office and she showed me the same "flag" that I had been shown before I left. Someone had faxed it to her. Who was the sender? The fax cover sheet said "Snoopy."

She said, "I don't know what's going on but you won't be able to stay in the course if you don't get this fixed." I understood and went out to my car and got on my phone. I already had the contact information of the Judge Advocate General for the New Jersey Army National Guard (ARNG) saved in my phone, just in case. I called him and told him what happened and explained that if it wasn't fixed that I wouldn't be able to stay. I presented the information and waited for resolution. By 1600 that afternoon, I was called back to the First Sergeant's office. She had received what was needed: a flag removal. It was signed by the Chief of Staff of the NJ ARNG. This is significant because when a simple flag is issued by a Unit Commander, that Commander would be the one to remove it. I was quite astonished that my own previous Commander did not remove his own flag. I wound up graduating ANCOC with 100% GPA.

It was time to make my escape again. For me, I wasn't in a stable, peaceful environment so I needed to find a new duty assignment. I was tired of performing for these people and still being treated horribly. I decided that I had three options: Drill Sergeant, overseas deployment, or federal Title 10 AGR. I was going to work all three options at the same time and take the first train smoking.

This E7 female at National Guard Bureau (NGB), who was supposed to be processing my AGR packet was not helpful at all. All she needed to do was make sure it was completed and pass it on to the Division Sergeant Major. She kept saying she was missing documents that I had clearly sent her.

A while later, I called NGB to check on the status of my packet. This same female was still giving me the run around, so I hung up on her. But she called me back. I just wanted my packet to leave her desk and she clearly had a problem doing that. I got tired of the back and forth, so I decided to take my entire personnel file and just show up to her office. I took a two-day pass and drove to Arlington, Virginia. As soon as I got there, I took my files, found her desk, walked up to her, and asked her, "Now what do you need?" It turns out that she had everything she needed after all. She promptly processed my packet and sent it to forward for review and approval.

Kenny J Productions

While military life kept trying to push me down, my dancing life was raising me up. I was still going to soul line dance classes in my spare time and going to soul line dance events on the weekends. Now that I was about to move, I needed to figure out how to keep track of all the dances I'd learned, so I started recording the ones that I liked. Every now and then, I'd figure out how to record myself dancing, but that wasn't important.

One of the classes I attended was in Philly and in the middle of class someone came in through the door. All I could think was, "In walks the sunshine." In came this man dressed in bright sunshine yellow, head to toe. I later found out that it was his favorite color. After class was over, he introduced himself. He told me had a dance group called I Am Kenny J Productions (IAKJP) and wanted to know if I was interested in joining his performance dance team called Sophisticated Funk. I had never heard of them before, but I was open to it since I had danced and performed before. I started taking classes with Kenny J and we started rehearsing for our next performance.

Even though I was moving to another state soon, I still felt obligated to the team. Kenny and I talked about options and decided he would record my part of the performance and send it to me so I could practice. Once I learned it, I drove back to New Jersey to rehearse with the rest of the team. I went back and forth two or three times and perfected my place in the routine. It was easy to manage because I was a quick learner and I always knew that my place was next to or opposite the other shortest person on the team, Connie English (RIP).

When it came time to travel to Indianapolis for the United We Dance Soul Line Dance Convention, a lot of us in IAKJP decided to coordinate our travel plans so we could fly out of the same airport around the same time. Of course we wore our IAKJP red, black, and white attire, and we could see each other all through the airport. One of the members brought a music player and we found time to even do some line dancing at the gate. The flight I was on was full of IAKJP members. One of the flight attendants invited us to show her a few steps and we did, right there in the aisle.

My first performance with IAKJP was not only fun but it also solidified to me that I was welcomed into a family who cared about me and enjoyed having me around.

Eventually I received my orders to move to Virginia and I had all of these videos but I didn't know where to put them. When I learned about YouTube, I loaded all the videos I had recorded just to have a place where I could find them and practice, but I had to come up with a name to start an account. All I could come up with was Petite Princess. I thought it was corny, but no one would know it was me anyway. In 2006, I created my YouTube channel, PetitePrincess92 and started uploading my videos. I don't know how because I didn't advertise it and I didn't want anyone to know it was me, but people found my channel.

Later, I saw a channel created by a friend and nationally known choreographer, Bernadette Burnette, which had her photo on it. Seeing this made it okay for me to come out of my shell. The name Petite Princess stuck, and even though people didn't really know my real name, they somehow found out it was me. I would show up to the parties and people would speak to me, "Hey, Petite!"

| 8 |

Working on My Best Self

When I moved to Virginia in 2006 to work at NGB, that would be my first time working around a lot of females, which I knew was going to be a challenge for me. I was consciously thinking about this. Females are very emotional and that was something I wasn't used to. What I believed about females was based on what the guys I had worked with were telling me. I had some really good friends who were females, but there were also those who were not desirable. In this new environment, I knew I had to make adjustments on how I dealt with them specifically. How would I deliver information so that they'd receive it? How would I receive information from them without being irritated or annoyed? How would I maintain my own emotional control when dealing with them? Not everyone required this much focus but for those it applied to, it could be very challenging on both parts.

"A sender with no receiver is just a noisemaker."—Erinn Watkins

Being my best self

It seemed military life kept wanting to push me down, but I knew I wanted to keep working on becoming my best self. Early on in my career, I never knew what my best self was. At the time, it was something between "don't make a mistake" and "don't let anyone take advantage of you." I knew I was valuable, so I fought to make sure they knew it too. I knew that I wanted to go to college. So, I needed to get a degree. I needed to work on my physical fitness. There were several blocks that I needed to check on my NCOER, so to keep myself focused and to motivate me to push through the hard times, I decided I wanted to do the things that improved what I looked like on paper.

One of my goals was to get a 300 on my PT test. Ever since I could remember, I wanted to have an APFT Excellence in Fitness patch, which was issued to everyone who maxed their PT test. The best I had gotten before setting this goal was a 290. I began to think that I could definitely get 300 if I had already gotten 290. When I was at NGB, they put up a banner with all the names of the people who had 300s. Because I wanted my name on that banner, I decided I would try again. Six months later, I was scheduled to take another APFT. I used to get so anxious before a PT test. I always did well but I was still terribly anxious every time. One day, I decided that I would rehearse in my mind what I was going to do ahead of time instead of waiting until I got to the PT location. I would go over each event, start to finish in my head. I knew what I was going to do before I got there. I had a predetermined number of push-ups and sit-ups I was going to do based on my last score. And I knew what my run needed to be based off of that. I discovered that if I adjusted one event, the other events were affected. So I manipulated my score ahead of time in order to figure out what I needed to score in each event in order to get what I wanted.

After completing the push-ups and sit-ups, all I had to do was the run. I mentioned to a Sergeant Major who was taking the test as well that I was trying to get a 300 that day but I was worried about the run. We all took off at the same time, and as I was coming in the last stretch, that same Sergeant Major came and ran with me. He pushed me through to the finish. I got a 300. They had already taken the banner down, but that was okay, I got my 300 and I was happy anyway.

So, being your best self means setting goals for yourself and figuring out a way to push through. Almost every school I attended in the military taught me that you have to figure out a way to make the mission happen. I did that, but I never got to my ultimate best self. I was always striving to get there. As soon as I made time to work on myself or do some great and wonderful thing, I had to set that aside to deal with the foolishness around me. When you look at my accomplishments, it may seem like I did a lot, but I hadn't really gotten started yet. I always felt I had never done enough, that I had so much more to offer. Just imagine what I could have accomplished without all the distractions. The people who bullied and otherwise harmed (or attempted to harm) me were distracting me from my own greatness, but I was already running circles around people without even trying. The sky was the limit for me.

This is one of the regrets I still struggle with. And try as I might, there's nothing I can do to go back and fix it.

Personnel Division and volunteer opportunities

To continue working on myself, I wanted to work at a higher level and be more involved in volunteer work. The job I applied for at the NGB was to work in the GIS department. Since I had already spent years working on the Civil Support Teams, this would be a step up for me, and I wanted to work at a higher level. When I got there, a Black female Sergeant Major scooped me up and assigned me to work for her in Personnel Division.

Initially I looked up to her but that soon changed, as she seemed to always come at me for something. She sometimes accused me of not working hard enough even though my desk was at a window that looked into the interior of the building and people could see I was at work. I also hardly ever left my desk yet, somehow this wasn't enough.

When I arrived at Personnel Division, I learned that the department had been working on a new system to help manage all personnel
assigned to the NGB, which included civilians as well as Soldiers. They
had been working on this project for at least a year, but they weren't
getting very far. I was invited by a Lieutenant Colonel to attend one
of the meetings held by the division leadership with the programmers
where the programmers would take notes and build what they thought
the department wanted. However, the back and forth was lost in trans-
lation. Since I used to build websites as a hobby, I thought that I could
interpret what they wanted in the form of a website and give that information to the programmers who could build the request from there.
So that's what I did. The Division bought me a laptop and the software
I needed. At my desk, I had my regular desktop computer where I did
my actual job, but then I had a laptop I was using to build this website.
The Black female Sergeant Major refused to allow me time to work on
this project,so I just had to fit it in when I could. The programmers
worked in the cubicles right next to me so I could go talk to them at
any time. Six months later, they had a functioning system ready for use.
We started manually adding all the hundreds of AGR Soldiers' orders
into this new system. It was a lot of work.

Part of my responsibility in Personnel Division was to manage the
Sergeant Major/E9 Promotion Board, so all the Title 10 AGR E8s submitted their promotion packets to me. While going through the Soldiers' files, I noticed something strange about all the promotion dates.
At first, I couldn't put my finger on it, but the following year, it stuck
out like a sore thumb. Many promotion dates were wrong. They had
been using the wrong data field which meant that a lot of the Soldiers
missed out on being promoted on time. I presented my findings to my
boss, the Sergeant Major, but to my knowledge, she did nothing with
the information.

I spent my time between working on this new personnel management system called Human Resources Management System, or HRMS,

and doing my regular job of managing the personnel files of my portion of the alphabet, which was P through Z. I took care of my people. I treated their records as if they were my own. Sometimes, when other leaders came to NGB they would bring me gifts. I was particularly fond of the gifts left by an unknown Special Forces soldier: a pocketknife, calculator, and shirt. I displayed these items on my desk because I was proud of them, but someone stole my pocketknife.

I knew the new HRMS system so well that I was invited to brief the Senior Enlisted Conference held in Germany. When it was my turn to get up and speak, I introduced myself and I wanted them to put a face to the person who had been managing their files for the past two years. So I asked the audience, "Where are all my P through Zs?" They clapped, laughed, cheered, and raised their hands, which felt really good.

While working at NGB, we regularly received requests for volunteers for different things around the Capital region. Military personnel who pass away have certain benefits. One of them, if authorized, is to be buried at Arlington National Cemetery. In order for this to take place, military members who are selected as Casualty Assistance Officers are assigned to help the family get through this difficult time. I was fortunate to have had the opportunity to perform this duty on three occasions while assigned at NGB.

The first time was pretty straightforward. It was a Soldier who had been killed during the Korean War and was repatriated as the result of DNA identification. I had to meet him, in his casket, at the airport at the gate, ensuring that it was deplaned and placed in the hearse. I then escorted the soldier to the funeral home, ensuring that he was taken care of there. I was on standby for the next of kin, a person designated by the soldier, for the entire time they were in town. I made sure that anything this person needed was provided. The second time was for a soldier who had been killed in Afghanistan. I remember the mom didn't want to be involved in any of it, so I dealt mainly with the father. For me it was emotionally difficult. Even though it was a sad occasion, you have to be perfect and professional in order to ensure the family has the best final memory of their loved one.

Another opportunity was for volunteers to help organize the first Operation Warrior Gauntlet. It was easy for me to do because I had already been a Training NCO and my experience as an Operations NCO was exceptionally valuable. There are certain individual tasks, called Warrior Tasks, that all soldiers are required train on. Soldiers who find themselves assigned to NGB weren't really equipped and encouraged to accomplish this training. The purpose of Operation Warrior Gauntlet was to correct this gap for all soldiers assigned to the National Capital Region.

I had another opportunity to shine. NGB wanted to conduct a simulated mass casualty event and needed someone to organize it. Using my experience on the Civil Support Teams, for me it was a piece of cake.

Social life

When I moved to Virginia, I wanted to start socially line dancing again, but I wasn't sure where to find line dancers. Someone once told me that if you find the "hand dancers" (an improvisational form of swing style partner dancing), you'll find the line dancers. So that's what I did. I looked for a local D.C. hand dance event.

I was still performing with Kenny J and Sophisticated Funk in different locations in Maryland and Virginia. There was one competition in Virginia where the DJ played different types of music in between competitions. What I didn't recognize at the time was that the music that was played was particular to a style of dance. One style I saw couples doing fascinated me. I remember wondering, "How does the lady know where to go?" That style was called Chicago steppin'.

Chicago steppin', originally called bopping, goes back to the late 1940s and early 1950s. The dance is done in either a six-count or eight-count beat. The follower travels up and down the lane, and the follower steps in and out of the lane. Both the leader and the follower use the basic count to create their own steps called "footwork."

D.C. hand dancing and Chicago steppin' were two dance styles that I immediately wanted to learn: that very month I started taking classes in both styles. I found a local dance club in Maryland where I could practice my skills. It was the perfect location because you could hand dance on one side and Chicago step on the other side. You had to know how to start the dance and you had to know the count and tempo, which was quite challenging. But I wanted to learn it, so I did.

Even at work, I wanted to share how much fun I was having with dancing. During the Christmas parties at NGB, I invited my soul line dance friends to come and teach soul line dancing to my colleagues and their families. I later started my own dance group, DMV Fuzion, and started teaching classes. I even created several line dances of my own.

Since I was dancing, I took my son to these dancing events as well. We used to have a competition between us to see who could stay on the floor the longest, which meant that we had to learn the steps on the floor. Sometimes I won and sometimes he won. I also taught him social dancing; I taught him how to hand dance and how to step.

One year I found out about an all-dance cruise. I had always wanted to go on a cruise, but I never wanted to be stuck on a boat with nothing I liked to do. A friend of mine was a Chicago steppin' instructor on the cruise, so I went with her and we shared a room. Bell Biv Devoe, one of my favorite groups growing up, were on the cruise, and I especially enjoyed their choreography.

While in the third row from the stage, I started dancing in the aisle. Even though I had heels on at the time, I was matching all of their steps. It was a lot of fun. At a break in their performance, one of the members asked, "Is there anyone who would like to come up on stage?" I looked around and watched several ladies go up. But then he asked again, "Is there anyone else who would like to come up on stage?" He turned a looked in my direction. Surely, he wasn't thinking of me. I backed up and blended back into the crowd. I couldn't do it.

I decided to go on the same cruise again the following year. My son had never been, so I bought us both a ticket this time. The year after that, I bought us tickets again but I was feeling extremely anxious about it. I decided to send him on the cruise with my nephew, Jordan Bell(RIP), who was a senior in high school by then. I thought of it as his graduation present. My son was twenty-five at the time. I knew all of the instructors on the cruise and picked two of them who kept an eye on them on the trip. They had a great time!

I also started running as a hobby. I didn't feel like a runner, but I decided to try my first 5k. It was a strange mental challenge because I wanted to stop at two miles, but I knew I wasn't done yet. I had to keep going. This was a result of the many years of running two miles for the APFT. I decided to find a local running group, but I didn't want to look out of place. I decided to find their schedule and drive by their next meeting location just to see what they looked like. I got there and they looked like regular people. So I decided that the first thing I would do is at least look like a runner. I bought a new running outfit with coordinated shoes and accessories. I showed up and no one cared whether I was a runner or not. Everyone was so friendly. I was hooked. I later ran my first distance race, the Army 10-Miler, and then ran another one the following year. Since then, I've run several other races, including two marathons.

Hostile work environments

While my social life, working in the Personnel Division, and volunteering helped me work on my best self, hostile work environments constantly kept me from meeting my goals and getting to my best self. Isn't that always how it is? When you have goals that you've set for yourself, there will always be obstacles along the way, but you still have to figure out a way to get things done.

What you can also do is decide that you don't want to be in the situation that you're in and do something about it. If you don't, then nothing will change. Once you acknowledge your situation and do nothing about it, you're deciding to stay where you are from that point on. You're taking responsibility for and ownership of your own circumstances, whether you like it or not.

For me, going along to get along wasn't an option. If I were in a bad place (especially due to others), I didn't think I deserved it. I would internalize, "Is this me?" I would look in the mirror and ask, "Well, what am I doing that's causing all of this?" I was the common denominator. Once I asked myself if I was doing my best, I concluded that it wasn't me. It was the people around me and I had to do something about it. I had to find a way to manage the hostility and make them leave me alone.

The Sergeant Major who was my boss never really left me alone. Finally I went to the Equal Opportunity office and complained about this hostile work environment. They must've called her when I was on my way back to my desk because she called me into her office as soon as I returned. She said, "Since you think this is a hostile work environment, I'm sending you to Arkansas in 30 days." I was not scheduled to move and Eric had just started school. Another Sergeant Major had previously warned me about her, saying "Be careful; she'll send you to Timbuktu." I went back to the EO office where they informed me that this was retaliation, and I was assigned to another Division altogether.

I was an E7 when I reported to my new duty assignment which was J-3 Directorate in Crystal City, VA. The Division Sergeant Major gave me my initial counseling as expected. However what wasn't expected was what he said to me: "You know I live across the street. We can go play naked poker." How do you answer that? Just like in PLDC, I had to think carefully about my response. The E8 promotion board was coming up in a few months. How could I say no without saying no? Would he do something to jeopardize my chance of being promoted? I had no idea. I remember being stunned. It was so shocking to me that I don't remember what I said, if anything at all. I must have handled it okay because, several months later, I got promoted anyway. And with that promotion, I was moved to another Division.

One day, I confided in my new Division Sergeant Major, Sgt Major Manuel Adams, about how I was feeling and what had been happening to me. I came to him complaining about a problem I was having. He told me something profound. He replied with one simple word. Good. "But they're doing this thing to me, Sergeant Major. Why me?" He replied, "Why not you?" And walked away. It stopped me in my tracks. I thought, how inconsiderate. Didn't he care about what happened to me? He did. What he was telling me was to take advantage of adversity and use it as an opportunity.

In other words, when negativity comes my way, accept it with full force, wide open arms, and absolute confidence. Opportunities kept coming my way. I was chosen to do job after job despite what I looked like.

Being the best leader I could be

Though the work environment had some hostile moments, I focused on being the best I could be, like always, and I was promoted to Master Sergeant/E8 in July 2009. The promotion meant I had to be moved from J-3 Directorate in Crystal City to a new position commensurate with my rank. When you get promoted, there's a tradition that you have a ceremony to celebrate your promotion and get pinned in front of your colleagues, family, and friends. When I made E8, I had a lot of anxiety about planning my ceremony and thought, Maybe somebody will do it for me. Not only did nobody do it, but nobody offered either. So, for two weeks I walked around as an E7 because I hadn't pinned on my rank yet. I finally decided, I didn't need a ceremony, and I just pinned on my own rank.

When I began walking around with my E8 rank on, a Lieutenant Colonel who ran the Division I belonged to, who knew that I hadn't yet had a ceremony, came up to me and asked, "What are you doing? That promotion isn't for you. That's for other people to see." That was true. I needed to be promoted in front of everyone, especially the junior Soldiers so they could see that someone who looks like them can make it to that level. I was a role model and didn't realize it. Even though I didn't have that ceremony because I felt it was too late, that was a lesson I haven't forgotten.

When I arrived in my new position, I decided I would take the normal thirty days to see how things worked, and then I would make adjustments where I felt they were needed. I had two Soldiers who worked for me. One was a SSG/E6 and the other was a SSG/E6 . The male was a very intelligent young man. He was well-liked and performed his job very well. The only problem I had with him was that he wasn't working a full workday. He came and left when he wanted. He took excessive lunch breaks and sometimes would leave his desk during the day and not come back until it was time to go home. This was unacceptable to me, so I counseled him for it. I gave him explicit instructions on how we were going to operate and told him that we would revisit the matter in thirty days to check his progress. Do you know that he went and told on me? It was almost funny because what I did wasn't out of the ordinary. It was just that he had never been given structure. No one ever told him what he could and could not do. I called him my "Golden Child" who could do no wrong. He was that good at his job. But I needed a total Soldier.

I was called into my boss's office and he asked me, "What's going on? Why is this Soldier crying?" I had no idea he had cried about a counseling statement. He told my boss that I was out to get him, which

I wasn't. I explained my position and he understood. I kept my eye on the Golden Child and checked his progress on my requirements. Thirty days later, I counseled him again. That time, I told him I was proud of him and his performance and to keep up the good work. We got along great after that.

The female was the total opposite. She was a great Soldier. Her only issue was that she lacked soft skills. She liked to interrupt people and she would do it all the time, no matter who was speaking. What was on her mind was more important than what was going on around her. I never thought she did this on purpose though. No one ever told her she needed to behave any differently. But since I was her leader, she was a reflection of me, and I couldn't allow her to continue being an example of poor professionalism.

I dealt with her differently than the Golden Child though. I made a list of some soft skills that I wanted her to work on based on my observations. I told her that I noticed that, when she needed something from me, she always interrupted, especially if I was on the phone. I knew if she was doing it to me, she was doing it to others as well. I didn't mind helping her, but I needed her to be more observant. When you go to someone's desk, look first, and see what they're doing. I know you have something on your mind that you have to get out, but you have to treat that thought like a hot potato. You just have to hold it. It was great. She got it. She went on to be an even better asset to our Section and the Division as a whole.

Besides our section's function of managing and processing line of duties (LODs) for the ARNG, another one of my responsibilities in this new position was to help respond to Congressional inquiries. Anytime someone submitted a Congressional request to their Congressman and the information requested dealt with our section, it was my job to immediately stop what I was doing, no matter what time of day, and research and submit our department's response to the inquiry that would be used to draft the overall response to the constituent.

NGB First Sergeant

While stationed at NGB, they created and assigned the very first Installation First Sergeant. I felt that this position was created so that NGB could function better as a real unit, even though we were in the Military District of Washington (MDW). After his tour was over, the second one was appointed. 1st Sergeant Kevin Matthews previously was a Master Fitness Trainer, which appeared to be the route to promotion to Sergeant Major: MFT, 1SG, then promotion to Sergeant Major.

1st Sergeant Kevin Matthews was very helpful to me. I looked up to him a lot. He was a good mentor and provided me with a lot of good advice. Once this second First Sergeant's tour was up, I decided to put my name in the hat. After all, I had shown my leadership capabilities well. I submitted a packet to be the next NGB Installation First Sergeant because I knew I could handle it. One day I went to the Chief of NGB's office and before I left, someone who worked there had something to show me. It was a list of all the Title 10 E8s. I hadn't seen anything like it before. It was an order of merit list and my name was at the top of the list. I had no idea. How did they know? How did anyone know who I was and what I could do? All this time, and after all I had done, I still didn't feel I was doing anything special. I didn't feel like I was doing enough.

I submitted my packet and waited for the results. The First Sergeant called me into his office and gave me the news. He said, "How'd you like to be the next NGB Installation First Sergeant?" I was so honored. He asked if I had a minute to go and speak with the Chief of Staff. Of course I did. We both went to his office and he asked me a few questions. "Do you think you can handle the job?" "Yes sir!" I said. Afterward, I went back to my desk and waited for the mass email announcing to all of NGB who their next Installation First Sergeant was going to be. A week went by, and then another. Nothing. Then the email I was waiting on announcing the new First Sergeant came. Only it wasn't my name they announced. It was someone else. And yes, it was a white male.

I couldn't believe it at first—but then I could. Someone snatched from me what was truly supposed to be mine. But how? One day I was walking through the office and an officer approached me. This person actually worked in the Boards Section. She told me that even though the results had already come out, this newly appointed First Sergeant hadn't submitted a packet so they re-held the board. I filed an IG complaint after that and all of my issues were founded. There was still nothing I could do to fix it. Whoever this person was, he still would never be better than me. I was the best and I had already proved it.

One day, one of my soldiers came to me and said this new First Sergeant tasked him to work on a project. That was a huge no-no in my book. If anyone wanted any of my Soldiers for anything, they needed to check with me first and that hadn't happened. So I went directly to speak to the First Sergeant and asked him what this was all about. After he gave his answer, I advised him that my soldier would not be working on any outside projects because he already had enough work to do, which was true. I also advised him that at any time if he needed to task my soldier with anything, he needed to see me first. NO ONE comes between me and my soldiers. I never had any further issues.

One day, this First Sergeant called a meeting with all the NCOs. We filed into a huge conference room and I found a seat in the back. He started off by talking about duty, honor, and respect. I couldn't listen to him so I walked out. Later on someone told me that he actually made an announcement to the room about my departure. That was very trivial to me and indicative of a leader letting his emotions get the best of him.

| 9 |

The Final Straw

One day as I was walking past Sgt Major Adams, he asked me, "Hey would you like to work at Fort Bragg? It's a position I used to work at and you'd be a good fit." I said, sure. I thought it would be good for me to get away from the "flag pole" and get back to the "real Army". I received my orders reassigning me to the National Guard Liaison at the US Army JFK Special Warfare Center & School (SWCS, pronounced "swick") at Fort Bragg, North Carolina.So I decided to drive down and find a place to stay. They called it "Fayette-nam." I was actually afraid, so much so that I remember driving around the base making notice of all the blue call boxes. Those are the ones people use to call the MPs in case of trouble. This turned out to be overblown anxiety, but I was cautious anyway. I was by myself and I needed to be aware of my surroundings.

When I took over at the National Guard Liaison office at Fort Bragg, there was no standard operating procedure on how to do that job. Every job in the military has or should have a standard operating procedure, but there was nothing in writing that I could refer to that explained how to do each task. The soldier I replaced had a fantastic way of running the entire office, which was a huge feat in and of it-self because he was not Admin. He was an 18C, an SF Engineer. For

National Guard Soldiers, there were so many moving parts to accomplish to get one thing done. He was so gracious to me. Every day I sat with him and just watched him do his thing. It was remarkable because everything was in his head. I even told him that I was going to take everything in his head and write it down on paper. He laughed.

I was responsible for taking care of the ARNG soldiers who came to SFQC, Special Forces Qualification Course. They all came through my office. I took care of their arrival, departure, pay, promotions, leaves, and passes among other things. I took care of everything that needed to be done so that the soldier could focus on his training. Promotions was huge because an SFQC graduate was automatically promoted to Sergeant pending board recommendation. A soldier could arrive as an E1 and leave as an E5 just by completing the course. Six months later, they could be promoted to E6. For ARNG soldiers it was not so cut and dry. I could promote any soldier all the way to E4 while he was in training, but it was up to his state to send those soldiers to a promotion board. I learned that one ARNG SFQC graduate was still wearing E4 rank at his home unit more than a year later only because he wasn't board recommended. This was unacceptable to me.

Since I was already familiar with the formal promotion board process from my time working at the 1/507th, I decided to start having a formal promotion board right there at the school so that requirement could be satisfied and the state would not have that reason to not promote those deserving soldiers. After all, they had earned it. Going before a promotion board meant that they were going from field duty to getting dressed up and having to report to a President of the Board, answer questions, and perform facing movements, I conducted sessions in my office for those guys who wanted to practice before the big day. I also inspected their uniforms if they wanted.

The most toxic environment

My first two years at SWCS went very well, but then in August 2014 it was time for a new boss. The bullying and toxic environment I started experiencing was absolutely psychological on a whole different level. I didn't realize it at the time, but what they were doing felt like pure evil. It just felt wrong. And I know for a fact that they were fascinated that I kept getting away or kept ahead of them. I distinctly remember the mind-boggling intimidation and tactics they used. The coercive tactics were so intense. But I was never helpless or hopeless and I always had faith in my individual capabilities. Threats didn't work because I never allowed myself to be controlled. I didn't care about any occasional indulgence. I could take it or leave it. I would not comply. I would always resist. Fort Bragg was so intense and difficult, but I asked for it. I cannot stress enough how massively mentally challenging it was for me. I had never experienced anything like it in my entire career. It had never been this bad. While I was going through it, it never dawned on me that I was increasingly being damaged in the process.

If I hadn't been toughened up by the time I had gotten to Fort Bragg, I don't think I would have survived like I did at all.

Conflict and confrontation

I treated those guys like I treated my son. I gave them much respect because just by being there they were on a whole different level than any ordinary soldier. One day I was informed that one of the students took off and went to D.C. without telling anyone. I don't know what he was thinking, but he came into my office and I asked him about it. He said he had to go see his newborn baby. I sat him down and told him, "You've got to let me help you." Wanting to see his child was certainly understandable. All he needed to do was tell me and I would've taken care of it.

When I was at work, sometimes other SF soldiers would come to my office and want to chat. If they wanted to talk, I'd immediately stop what I was doing, turn to them with all of my attention, and say, "What's up?" We'd talk about anything: religion, politics, girlfriends, or just idle chit chat. My door was always open. I didn't have to say it but they knew it. They could always come and talk to me about anything.

On another occasion, I had the unfortunate task of "locking heels." "Locking heels" is when an Officer or NCO gives a direct order to a subordinate to stand at attention or parade rest. The feet are planted in place for the duration until the person is relieved. Hence, locking heels. I hate having to do it and I've only done it twice in my entire career. As an E8, I gave this E3 specific instructions in order to help him with his pay issue and then report back to me the next day. He never came to see me, so the next time I saw him I asked him what happened. He said this SF E7 male who worked in our office told him he didn't have to. I said to him, "Do you realize I gave you specific instructions to take care of your problem and you chose to listen to the E7? Do you realize I outrank him?" I told him to follow me and we went upstairs. As we got to the top landing I stopped him—he was at least six feet two—and told him, "Get at parade rest! Do you understand that I'm the expert? I'm the one who's going to take care of your pay?" I never had another problem with him.

I did, however, have a problem with Sgt. Maj. Vinker, my new boss. One day everyone in our section went to lunch. It was all E7s, E8s, and him. As we all walked outside, I showed Sgt. Maj. Vinker my new car. I had just bought it in February 2015. He asked me what I did to get that car, suggesting that I'd had sex with the dealer to get it.

Since PLDC back in 1994, I had not quite been able to defend myself against sexual harassment for fear of retribution. This reminds me of the previous boss who asked if I wanted to play naked poker. But this time was different.

Since I worked at 4th Battalion, once I got back to the office , I immediately called SFC Zachary Weber. He was the 4th Battalion Sexual Harassment/Assault Response & Prevention NCO (4th BN SHARP). After this discussion, I decided that mediation was the course of action I wanted to take. The first person I called was Sgt. Maj. David Campbell. I chose him mainly because he's a peer of Sgt. Maj. Vinker and also because he was my previous boss before Sgt. Maj. Vinker. The mediation took place in the 4th BN Conference Room.

Initially Sgt. 1st Class Weber was going to do the talking, but I stopped him because I felt Sgt. Maj. Vinker needed to hear it from me. I was so fascinated that he apologized because he really didn't have to. He could've denied it because it was my word against his and he did so in front of all of his peers and colleagues. Upon hearing him apologize, I was satisfied with the outcome, and I felt that the incident was over.

I found myself being defiant with Sgt Major Vinker on another occasion. Both I and my solider, Sgt First Class Jamila Robinson, nearly missed out on an opportunity to participate in the 2015 Title 10 Promotion Board cycle. Because I used to work at NGB and part of my job included processing and managing promotion packets for all Title 10 E8s competing for promotion to E9, I had special insight on how the promotion board was supposed to go. While I was on leave, one of the Sergeant Majors, Sgt Major Joe Gerber, in our department came up with some arbitrary deadline. My soldier hadn't yet submitted her packet because she wasn't going to compete at first, but she still had time, so she submitted it to the Sergeant Major. anyway. Sgt Maj. Gerber replied to her saying she had missed his deadline. His deadline had no bearing on whether any soldier was able to participate in any promotion board. When I returned from leave, I saw this email traffic and, realizing that this was improper. So, I asked Sgt First Class Robinson to send me her NGB 4100 and I would submit both of ours together. The NGB 4100 is a form used by Army National Guard soldiers to calculate their promotion points based on the information in their personnel file. I received the same response my soldier received, that his deadline had already passed. After a couple of days of back-and-forth emails, that Sgt Maj. Gerber sent a mass email requesting all available promotion packets to be sent to him. During this time I also had a discussion with another ARNG Special Forces soldier in my section who advised me that another ARNG Special Forces soldier in our department had no idea about the promotion board. Even though our packets were sent to the Sgt Maj. Gerber for signature by the first O6 in our Chain of Command, we needed them returned so the entire packet could be forwarded to NGB. I sent my boss, Sgt Maj. Vinker, one final detailed email. I should've been an attorney for how precise it was. I explained my case using "if/then" statements. I copied all the Title 10 leadership in our department and every Title 10 Soldier in our department who could possibly be affected by this issue, inserted my closing statement, and then took a breath. I looked around for someone who could read it for me before I clicked "send." I searched, called but couldn't find anyone. My soldier was there but she was not senior enough. I walked out of the room. After a few minutes, I came back, opened the email, and clicked "send." I told my soldier, "Let's go to lunch."

While I was away at lunch, no one called me. When we returned from lunch, I checked my email, clearly expecting the storm to come raining down on me. But there was nothing. No reply, no response, nothing.

Sgt Maj. Gerber who denied our promotion packets relented and sent me the necessary documents, and we were all allowed us to turn in our packets. That Sergeant ended up being promoted to Staff Sergeant that year. If it hadn't been for me, he would've missed out.

This never should have happened. Sgt Maj. Vinker called me on the phone and wanted my reassurance that "this won't get out" and that "this won't go any further than this." I got what I wanted and that was to get our promotion packets submitted to NGB so I felt no need to push things any further. I did keep a mental note though. I would not forget.

Longest counseling

In 2015, as I was about to leave work, Sgt Maj. Vinker asked me to come over to his office for a few minutes. He wanted to talk to me so I went right over. What was supposed to be a few minutes turned into three hours, from 1700 to 2000. He had a blue folder in his hand and told me to walk with him to the conference room. It was me, him, and an ARNG SF Title 10 Major who worked in our department. Sgt Maj. Vinker decided he wanted to counsel me for something he said I did, but there was a reasonable explanation for what he thought and there were facts that he got just plain wrong. For everything he was telling me, I had supporting information to back up what I was saying, but it was back in my own office.

I became well aware that my job and my future in the T10 program were on the line. The nature of the counseling statement shows this. In this one counseling statement, Sgt. Maj. Vinker includes the entire time period since he became my rater, yet at no point in time had he ever counseled me on anything, let alone my job performance. He also includes things that happened months prior that had already been resolved.

He included things that he would've seen had been resolved if he'd asked about them. During this counseling session he also threatened me at least four times about my opportunity for promotion.

The climate in our office, among all the senior NCOs had by this time dramatically tanked. Two senior NCOs specifically were afraid of losing their jobs if they complained or voiced any negative concerns about what was going on. This was particularly important because, as the ranking NCO in the office, I was in a unique position to address all of our concerns to our leadership. I was already a Master Sergeant with more than 20 years of active duty, so my retirement was secure. There was nothing that could be held over my head, not even the threat of not being promoted, that could keep me from sticking up for all of us. I felt it was my responsibility and I felt obligated to do what I could to make work life better for all of us.

As I was sitting there in the conference room listening to Sgt Maj. Vinker talk, I was trying to keep track of everything he was saying because none of it was true. But he kept talking. I just wanted him to shut up so I could get to work writing my rebuttal. I had never in my life been in such deep thought and concentration and for such an extended period of time. Since I wasn't taking notes at the time, I had to keep track in my head of everything he was saying so I could rebut it, point by point. It was so intense. It must've shown on my face because periodically the SF Major, Maj. Danielson, would get my attention, and I would snap to look at him. It's as if he was snapping me out of a trance. He did this several times.

The first thing Sgt. Maj. Vinker said was that this was not a negative counseling, but it was. All the comments referred to "failure" to do something. I respectfully let him speak, but when it was time for me to provide my response, he kept interrupting me. This was very unnerving and intimidating, but I stayed focus and on point.

He kept mentioning me being potentially promoted to Sergeant Major. I feel that this was an attempt to use quid pro quo. If I just "play along" then I can be promoted to Sergeant Major. He mentioned it at least four or five times. This is when I really felt threatened.

I felt like he was trying to isolate me from my peers by attempting to turn us against each other. He kept mentioning one E8 as a source of conflict, but this was not true at all. We got along very well.

He brought up that I hadn't shown up to an exercise. The unit was having an exercise and needed volunteers to participate so I volunteered to be Document Custodian. The exercise location was to take place in Charlotte, North Caroline. Sgt. Maj. Vinker said that I decided not to show up, but this wasn't true. I spoke with two other E8s about where to report to. They both made calls on my behalf and we were never able to determine where I was supposed to report to in Charlotte. I was not about to drive all the way to another city and not know where to go. Sgt. Maj. Vinker said the reason I volunteered was so that I could get out of doing staff duty, but I was going to be released from the exercise in time to pull my own duty.

I knew I was going to write a rebuttal. I always do. But this time was different. Since he was going to waste my time, I was going to waste his. I asked for some scratch paper and started writing. He ended up leaving the room because I was taking so long. Good! Leave! Altogether, there were fourteen points I was keeping track of in my head. I wrote about eight pages, front and back, addressing each of his concerns. I numbered each page and included the total number of pages on each page. I did this just in case they tried to lose a page. After that, I never heard anything about that counseling session again.

I received my NCOER for that year from this same Sergeant Major who gave me the longest counseling session ever. He called it my initial counseling, which was actually supposed to take place within the first thirty days of him becoming my rater. Instead, he waited until I had already worked for him for an entire year, which is unheard of. I could've asked to be counseled but there was no issue with him until the sexual harassment incident. It was terrible. As an E8 competing for E9 I needed to look outstanding on paper. In my previous NCOER, I had received the top rating in all blocks except for one. This one I received made me look like I was tremendously substandard. It was something that would certainly hinder me from being competitive for this upcoming board. The way that NCOER read appeared very un-characteristic of my abilities and the work that I had done, which was a dramatic difference within the span of only a year. I did what's called a Commander's Inquiry. This is a process whereby a soldier can submit a complaint to their Commander regarding an unfair evaluation report. I ended up reporting him to the USAJFKSWCS IG and the US-AJFKSWCS Equal Opportunity office. I was actually a whistleblower. I couldn't believe it. In December 2015, the suspects were notified, including Sgt. Maj. Vinker.

Promotion issues

I had also requested to attend my next leadership course called "Battle Staff NCO Course." It's a course for NCOs assigned to, or projected to be assigned to, Battalion or higher coordinating positions. Since I could potentially be promoted to Sergeant Major, this course would be a requirement for me in my career progression. There was nothing particular about attending this course as it was expected for all E8s to attend, but my request to attend the course was ignored by leadership. Instead of forcing the issue, I decided it was more important to just get out of Fort Bragg and I could request to attend the course once I PCSed back to NGB.

Not only was I denied a leadership school, but I was also being denied leave. But there was one leave request that I had to fight for. My son Eric was due to graduate from college, and I was not about to miss his graduation if I could help it. At first, Sgt. Maj. Vinker was not going to approve my request, but he eventually did. I went and surprised Eric by also flying Erica and my nephew, Gabriel to witness as well.

Leaving my mark

Later on, an Maj Danielson encouraged me to build a MS Access database from scratch. He wanted me to build a system to help manage our National Guard Soldiers in training to replace what we were using because that system was just not enough to suit our needs. It was an Army system, not a National Guard system. At first, I said no because, although I had used MS Access before, it had been years and I was no longer very familiar with it. If you don't use it, you lose it. But then I told him I'd look over it and get back to him. It was a challenge for me, and I shall not be defeated. I first downloaded the personnel data so I could work with it. I figured out how to create data fields, how to link the data fields, and how to create and run reports. After I built the database from scratch, I started thinking of things I could add to it. I wanted to add more functionality.

Because I knew that my eventual replacement may not necessarily be Admin, I decided to make it as easy as possible for the next person to jump into the job. I wanted the entire process. . . all moving parts. . . to be as automated as possible. I created Word documents, templates, for each task that would need to be accomplished for the National Guard Soldiers who were assigned to us for training. These Word documents were linked into the database so they could be produced singularly or in multiples. After testing the database, I created a user guide, complete with screenshots, to help anyone learn how to use it. Every time I went through hostility and conflict, I told myself that I would come up with something that would make them remember me. I was always going to leave a legacy. I was always going to leave something behind that had my name on it and they would have to use it. And there was nothing they could do about it. That system was my legacy. Again, I left my mark.

While this mark was something everyone could see, I also left my mark on individuals. Sometime after I arrived and took over the shop, another female Title 10 Soldier arrived to work for me. She was a single parent and had never left home before, so for her to go out on a limb to come to a base like Fort Bragg, North Carolina, and work at the Special Forces School was a tremendous leap for her to make, and I admired her for doing so. She was way too passive, emotional, and indecisive, and I knew you couldn't be that way and survive in that environment.

I noticed she had problems exerting her authority, not only as a SFC but also as the subject matter expert. The males in the office didn't know her job, but she didn't conduct herself in that manner. She was constantly calling or emailing me asking for permission to do this or do that. It started to get annoying. So to fix the situation, I decided to move back to that office and assist where I could.

Instead of doing her work for her, I decided I would just be observant and see how she handled things. That way I could better understand how to help her. It turns out that she was making all the right decisions. She was just unsure of herself. One day, as I was sitting at my desk which faced hers, a SF student came in the office for something. As I was listening to the dialogue between the two of them, I could tell she was glancing in my direction seeking some sort of approval of what she was telling him. I said nothing. I just kept my head down and acted like I didn't hear anything.

So I worked on her. For a whole year, I stood by her side and provided her moral support. I wanted to help her build up her confidence and be more like the SFC/E7 that was expected. It worked. She was way better than expected, and she took on the job like the professional I knew she could be. My job was done and I moved back to my office in the Headquarters building.

In early 2016 I decided to start taking better care of myself, so I decided to seek mental health assistance. My method of fixing everything myself was not sustainable. I was offered an opportunity to participate in a program called IOP, or intensive out-patient therapy. It's a fancy term for group therapy.

What? I thought? We'd be sitting around in a circle singing kumbaya. But it was none of that.

| 10 |

Mental Health Challenges

Most of my military career was spent in a constant state of survival, similar to how a prisoner of war survives. I was constantly trying to gain my freedom. The enemy (the toxic leaders) used psychological torture techniques (harassment, hostile work environments, Biderman's Chart of Coercion) that caused me to constantly seek means of escape. Each successive duty assignment was a means of escape, except that with each one, it started all over again, with different captors each time. Like clockwork, I knew what needed to be done. The process was all in my head. I knew what I needed to do to escape because I had trained for it during the previous assignment. The captors (toxic leaders) all used the same tactics. Once I understood and could identify the tactics, I could defend against them. Rinse and repeat. The problem for me was that I did it so often that it was mentally and emotionally draining. I was exhausted. Fort Bragg was the final battle. The worst of the worst. Only I didn't know it was to be my final battle because I still had the will to survive. Keep in mind the environment I was in. Not only was I assigned to the Special Forces School, but Civil Affairs and PsyOps were co-located in the same building where I worked. I knew I just needed to leave Fort Bragg and get to my next duty assignment and then I'd be home free, but I didn't make it. I believe that my previous experiences (self-training) prepared me for Fort Bragg. I think I made it as far as I was supposed to go but every now and then I still find my-self going back to those days and reliving certain things to see if there could've been a different outcome.

Depression and survival

First Sgt Kevin Matthews told me I had high-functioning depres-sion, which is when you're depressed but still productive. He saw it in me. I don't know how he knew, but he said his daughter was the same way. One of the symptoms is having a persistent feeling of sadness or emptiness. I was sad all the time. Sometimes the sadness would just "fall from the sky." It would come out of nowhere. I was also anxious a lot. I hid it well, but I did break down a couple of times. Once, dealing with that female Sergeant Major who was my boss at my last location was so overwhelming that I ran out of her office crying. The last thing she said to me was, "We want the old Sgt. Watkins back." How could she say that when she was the problem? I think I was in disbelief that she was treating me so terribly.

I think the reason I didn't have the rest of the symptoms of high-functioning depression such as hopelessness or pessimism is because I had the will to survive.

In appendix A of the US Marine Corps *Survival, Evasion, and Re-covery* manual, Psychology of Survival, it says:

a. Be prepared:

(1) Know your capabilities and limitations.

(2) Keep a positive attitude. Lift yourself up.

(3) Develop a realistic plan.

(4) Anticipate fears.

(5) Combating psychological stress:

(a) Recognize and anticipate existing "stresses." (injury, death, fatigue, illness, hunger)

(b) Attribute normal reactions to existing "stresses." (fear, anxiety, guilt, boredom, depression, anger)

(c) Identify signals of distress created by "stresses." (indecision, withdrawal, forgetfulness, carelessness, and propensity to make mistakes)

b. Strengthen your will to survive with:

(1) The Code of Conduct.

(2) Pledge of allegiance.

(3) Faith in America.

(4) Patriotic songs.

(5) Thoughts of return to family and friends.

This is what I was doing. I knew I still had choices. I still had options. The answers were out there. I just needed to hang on a little while longer. I never gave up.

Saying I had high-functioning depression was interesting, but I didn't think I had a problem. But then I recalled the day in my previous job in Personnel Division, a colleague suggested to me that I was depressed and should talk to someone. She even went so far as to look up the number for me and wrote it down. As soon as she handed it to me, my face started leaking. I couldn't do it. She didn't hesitate. She got on the phone and called for me. Between the two of us, we were able to schedule me an appointment to speak to a counselor. I met with a couple of different counselors during this time, but I didn't really open up to them. Even though they were professionals, I didn't trust them. I did learn what depression was and that I was in fact, depressed and anxious and had PTSD.

It was very hard at first to acknowledge that I had struggles with mental health. To do so would mean accepting that I had a defect. I couldn't do that so easily. I was the fixer. I always had a solution to problems. If there's a problem, I have to fix it. There are problems everywhere you look, too many problems for one person to handle, anyway. But for me, every problem had to have an answer.

Looking back now, I can see I was alone, depressed, and exhausted by all of it.

When I was on the Civil Support Team in Tennessee, the guys recognized one of my coping mechanisms was eating Brach's candy corns. I used to keep a jar on my desk just big enough to hold one full bag. If I were having a good day, they could tell by observing my "Brach's candy corn meter." If my day was not going so well, I could kill one bag in a day. But sometimes I could kill one bag before lunch. They told me later on that when I was out of town, even though they ate my candy corn, they made sure the jar was full by the time I returned. I had no idea. They were so thoughtful that they even bought the right brand, Brach's. I never knew.

Of course, the candy was just a coping mechanism. It didn't fix the issue. If I couldn't fix a problem, I felt like a failure but I never gave up. I still tried to find ways to go back and fix it. But there was the one thing I couldn't nail down: I couldn't fix myself. Even today, there are times when I feel like I'm the same person I was before. But then there are times when I have these reminders that tell me, "You're not the same. You're a different person. Yes, you have a disability and, yes, it creeps in sometimes. You're on the other side of that now. This is your NEW NORMAL."

What I've learned since then is that struggling doesn't mean you're defective. Not having all of the answers doesn't mean that you're not intelligent. Dropping the ball every now and then doesn't mean that you're a failure. None of that means that you're unworthy or incapable. It means you're human.

It took many years into my career to do so, but I started doing things to help myself. I was already at the end of my career when I decided it was okay to put myself first. Anyone who has been in the military for any length of time knows about "mission first." This translates into skipping out on much needed medical care or even professional development. You don't want to be the one to leave your team hanging, the one to not pull your load. But you suffer for it. I remember consciously deciding that I wasn't going to think that way anymore because it would be hurtful to me and I wasn't going to hurt myself anymore. Even when I tried to cope by using alcohol, that only lasted a month because I realized I was only hurting myself. When I make a decision, it's done. The only difference this time was that I was making decisions that would benefit me.

Anxiety

Around this time, I didn't recognize how stressed I was but it was something that others saw in me. Certain people who recognized the signs knew that something was wrong and that I needed help. I remember the day when it hit me. I was on my way to my typical hostile work environment at NGB. I was constantly put into all kinds of intense situations. I lived about three miles from work and I started noticing that I was extremely anxious every morning. This is very important. I had been anxious thousands of times before, but this time was different.

As I became aware of this uncomfortable feeling, I decided to do something about it. That was a huge step for me. It was important to notice that feeling because now I can identify it. So I thought, "What are some things that I can do to help myself deal with this feeling right now? How do I know? What can I do? When will it happen again? If it happens again, what will I do? How will I handle it?"

That's when I started putting together a mental self-check. I learned to do this when I started running as a hobby. After a few miles I'd do a head-to-toe self-check. Was I thirsty? Did I need water? Did I have a cramp? Am I tired or am I injured? Can I keep going? When I got anxious and started doing this self-check, I would take my hands and feel my face to see if my cheeks felt warm. Then I would feel my forehead. If it was wrinkled, it was because I was in distress. When I look at people who are in distress, they raise their eyebrows, their forehead is wrinkled, or they widen their eyes. Then I noticed that my heart was racing. I was also gritting my teeth. Now that I was getting all these physical signs, I was able to tie them back into this feeling of anxiety.

Then I would think back to fifteen or twenty minutes before. How was I feeling then? Then I would think of the time it took me to get from there (when I wasn't anxious) to here (when I was anxious) and figure out what I could have done to fix "it."

It became clear that when I was on my way to work to a hostile environment, I would likely feel anxious. So knowing it was coming, I would go through my checklist of things I could do in the moment:

> I can relax my face.
>
> I can drink water.
>
> I can breathe. Take deep breaths.
>
> I can leave the room or take a break.
>
> I can listen to music. I can sing songs.
>
> I can play games on my phone.
>
> I can look around and identify things I see.

I also learned that there were some basic things I could do to help me be my best self even though I was dealing with hostilities that might not let up for a while. I needed to help my body take care of me:

Eat right

Get enough sleep

Drink water

Get exercise

Have a hobby

After a while, I learned that if I was not performing at my best, I was probably missing one, . So I would need to address that missing item. In New Jersey, I was missing a hobby, so I started dancing.

I didn't come up with this method from something I read or was told. I literally began listening to my body teach me what my anxiety was. Then I listened to what my body was telling me I needed to do to fix it. Going into work anxious wasn't going to help me at work, so I needed to fix that. So, the simple rule is that once you recognize that something wrong is happening, take action to address it. Just don't accept it. Be proactive. And be purposeful.

When I was gritting my teeth, I didn't realize it until my jaws were tired. I decided to start wearing a dental guard so that way I'd know when it was happening and I'd be more conscious of it. I had a tangible reminder instead of waiting for the subconscious to become conscious.

Anger

The constant harassment and hostile work environments I was subjected to contributed to my anger because I was forever trying to prove myself. I had to be perfect and make no mistakes. I was trying to get these toxic people to leave me alone so that I could be my best "Soldier self." But I could never get there. I would always have to set that aside and then deal with the foolishness that came my way. I was intensely angry about that.

Despite what my critics would say, I never considered that the hostility I was experiencing was due to what I looked like which I couldn't change. I just always thought I was dealing with idiots. I would usually say to myself, "What in the entire hell is wrong with you people? Why can't you just do the right thing? Why can't you just do your d*** job?" This is the frustration I felt when I wanted to raise my fists above my head and pound them onto my desk. I was conscious of the stereotype regarding the "angry Black female" that I didn't want applied to me. I tried very consciously to not fit that stereotype. This what initially made me hold all my emotions inside. To me, that was a distraction from my greatness. I never had to force my way in. I just needed to be present, on time, in the right uniform with the right equipment. I needed to do my job, do it well and let my work speak for itself. But they were always looking for things that would validate their thinking, yet I never wanted to give them any confirmation.

It couldn't be the "angry Black female" stereotype because I was consistently mindful of my tone. When I was angry, I used to practice this exercise at my desk. I would close my eyes and do a self-check. If my cheeks were warm and my face was wrinkled. I would literally tell myself, "Relax your face. Relax your face."

Once, I noticed that I wasn't as good at hiding my emotions as I thought I was. I discovered this when I took my one of my last DA photos. A soldier's DA photo or Department of the Army photo is the official photograph in a soldier's personnel file. During my appointment, the photographer was cordial and professional. I knew I didn't want to smile. After reviewing so many promotion packets and so many DA photos, I knew in my mind that a smile can be taken any kind of way by a board member, so I wanted no distractions. I just wanted a pleasant look on my face. So to achieve this, I thought of my favorite food: sweet potatoes. But in the back of my mind, I felt disgusted that the people I worked for wouldn't leave me alone. I was standing there for my photo, looking good in my uniform. But in a few short minutes, I had to return to the chaos.

I received notice that my new photo was posted in my records. That's when I saw it. I was horrified. I looked at my hands in the photo. Instead of the relaxed placement of my hands alongside my uniform, my hands were balled up in fists. I basically told on myself and couldn't take it back.

This photo helped me begin to see how angry I was, and group therapy brought it all home. I was angry, but I didn't know how angry. Everything had always been internal. I remember sitting at my desk at work and knowing how bad my supervisor was treating me, I wanted to pound his head into the pavement, but I couldn't show it on my face. No one ever knew how angry I was or how much turmoil I had inside. I was even prescribed medication, specifically for anger, to help me calm down.

I used to call my anger my "Incredible Hulk." In lots of pictures of The Incredible Hulk, he's standing there enraged with his hands over his head like he's about to flatten someone or something. I felt the same way, except I could never complete the motion of pounding my hands onto the table because I always held it in. I never wanted anyone to be distracted by my emotions, so I didn't show them.

"You wouldn't like me when I'm angry." If I were angry enough, I couldn't speak. In fact, I would tell the fellow soldiers I worked with that I was good as long as I was talking. If I'm not talking, then it's not good. Watch out because I was on fire inside.

In group therapy we were asked to draw a picture of what anger looked like. I hated drawing, and I told them that I only do stick people. Everyone else picked up colored pencils and crayons, and I just sat there not knowing what to do. So I picked up one black pencil and I drew a picture of a head with no face and a body with no legs and no hands.

That's how I saw myself. After I drew it on paper "The Incredible Hulk" went away. I haven't seen it since.

But I had to learn to let go of my anger.

Self-isolation and underproducing

When it comes to anger, you have to put it somewhere. If it stays bottled up inside you, it's going to come out. It will either express itself as overproductive or underproductive. Mine was underproductive. I stopped going places and doing things I enjoyed. Once I even stayed home for two months straight. At the time, I had a roommate and the only reason I left my room was because I ran out of food. The worse it got, the more I retreated into myself. As I noticed this retreat, I would break out my coping mechanisms to bring myself back to my most productive self; however, this was getting more and more difficult to do as time went. My trusted tricks weren't working anymore, and it was getting harder and harder to bounce back.

A female officer, a Major, said three words to me: "Stay plugged in." Then she kept walking. That caught me off guard. I wondered, "What does that mean? Did she notice something about me that I was doing or not doing?" I finally figured out that it meant I shouldn't be isolated, that I need to stay plugged in to what's going on. Whatever it is, I need to know. I also understood later on that it meant it was important to be plugged into society and my environment, and that I don't have to stay to myself. That I should do things that involve other people. Talk to other people and find other like-minded people who I could associate with. That, to me, was staying plugged in. Staying plugged into society was one way that helped me deal with self-isolation. I found groups that I enjoyed, so that's how I stayed connected. I joined running groups and Facebook groups that were built around the things I liked to do, such as dancing and fitness.

When I got to Fort Bragg, my depression got worse, and I found myself underproducing, which lead to isolation. I was no longer plugged in.

I started spending a lot of time in my car, just sitting there. Contemplating or thinking or strategizing or listening to music. It was my safe space. But this turned into an unhealthy habit. zNow that my depression was getting worse, Fort Bragg is where I started having panic attacks.

Therapy

There are people out there who are paid good money to help you get through whatever you're dealing with. Use them. Make them work for their money. The first therapist, doctor, or counselor might not be the perfect fit, but you have to keep trying until you get what you want.

When you have mental health challenges, seeing any kind of health practitioner can be a challenge. I didn't want them to treat me like I was crazy, as if I didn't have any sense. I also didn't trust them because up until I started getting help, I only had my own thoughts to relate to. I wasn't talking to anybody. So, having to share what I was thinking with someone else and having to trust that they were going to take care of me or treat me right meant that I had to rely on that person, but I had been relying on myself up until this time, and that was hard to let go of. But I had been offered this opportunity to go to group therapy. So all day, every day for three months, my place of duty was a forty-minute drive from home. For the first thirty days, I didn't think I had a problem. My position was that I would simply participate by being there. At least no one could say that I didn't try. I didn't have to talk, so I didn't. In my mind, the other people had issues, not me.

Then on day thirty-one, the lightbulb came on. What they were telling me started making sense.

Talking to someone else ended up helping a lot. Group therapy helped because I was with others who I could identify with. In group therapy, you don't feel like you're alone or the only one dealing with mental health issues. You can see other regular people who have gone through the same or a similar thing, and you can help each other out. Certain medications had their place, specifically the medication for anger, but the talking was more helpful.

Micro agreements

One thing that helped with my anxiety was to use micro agreements. When you really think about it, we use micro agreements all the time. They're what get us through the day. When we decide to go to the store, we agree that we can go to the store and we do it. It's so seamless and happens so fast that we don't even notice it. But as my depression got worse, these micro agreements became fewer and fewer. I couldn't agree to do certain things anymore, and the list of things I couldn't do started to grow.

I remember the first time I used micro agreements to get myself beyond a moment of anxiety. I was in group therapy at the time and I would drive to the location and when it was over, I would drive home. Do not pass go. Do not collect $200. I was afraid to deviate from that. It wasn't safe for me for no other reason but that I couldn't agree to do anything else but that.

I was 30 days into the program and I felt like they weren't telling me anything I didn't already know. I didn't have a communication problem. I wasn't outwardly angry or emotional. I was already doing everything they were teaching. So for 30 days, I went to class and went straight home. And then one day I mentioned to the group that I was afraid to do anything beyond going straight home, which was important. It was step one: notice the thing.

From that moment on, I started getting more out of my therapy. While I was in treatment, I not only learned things for myself, but I also took the opportunity to use my experiences to reach out to others who were also in treatment. I noticed that I had additional perspectives that were beneficial to some of the patients—real life experience and practical application of what we were being taught. I discovered that what I had been doing for most of my life was called "coping," therefore I was in a unique situation that positively affected staff as well as those in treatment.

At some point, after step one, I remember determining what I could agree to do to fix my behavior, because I always thought I could fix anything so I could certainly fix myself. I decided I could check the mail on my way home. This meant that I had to deviate from doing something that was comfortable to doing something that was uncomfortable. I lived in an apartment complex, so the idea of checking the mail sounds pretty simple. It was simple, but for me it was a challenge nevertheless. Step two was to visualize yourself doing the thing. I rehearsed the task of checking the mail in my mind. I was able to complete the circuit: on the way home, stop by the mailbox, and then go home. I rehearsed this in my mind for a while until I just did it one day. I was able to continue to agree until I finally took action and accomplished the task. The fact that I didn't say no to the task meant that I agreed with myself that I could do it.

Another time, I decided that I wanted to go to the commissary. I drove there and parked my car, but that's as far as I got. I couldn't agree to go in the store. So I decided to visualize the steps I would need to take to get from my car and through the store, including which aisles to get which thing, through the checkout, and back to my car. I rehearsed this in my mind, but that's as far as I got. I went home. Several times I went to the parking lot, rehearsed the steps, and then went home, but I was eventually able to do it. I took action.

Taking action took three steps. My list of things I could agree to do was pretty simple but having a list with no progress made me feel like a failure and I needed to feel successful.

Step 1: Notice the thing

Step 2: Visualize yourself doing the thing

Step 3: Take action

Any disagreements just meant that I needed to add more steps. Add as many steps as you need to in order to get you to your desired end state. I had steps for everything. That came from my experience in flight school. Everything had a checklist. I needed structure, organization, no surprises. Again, using the example of going to the store, I broke that task down into steps or micro agreements.

Step 1: Drive to the store

Step 2: Park the car

Step 3: Lock the car door

Step 4: Go into the store

Step 5: Grab a shopping cart

Step 6: Go to the aisle and get the thing (I had specifics)

Step 7: Go to the checkout

Step 8: Pay for groceries

Step 9: Return to car

I literally rehearsed this entire process in my head until I could accomplish it, which was Step 3: Take action.

Learning to say no

You have to advocate for yourself even if it's just to say something as simple as, "No, I don't like that" or "No, I don't want to do that." It's hard to say no, but I learned how to do it through therapy. I had said no before and ended up suffering consequences, which made it even harder to say. Practice until you can say it. This is important because many times victims of sexual harassment or sexual assault are asked, "Did you say no?" If you didn't say "no," you're looked at differently. As if you caused your own trauma, as though it were your fault. If you didn't say "no," then you asked for it. You wanted it.

But what if you can't? What if the words just won't come out? It took me twenty-five years to be able to say the word "no." "No I don't want to do that." So what did I do all those years? I learned to say "no" without saying "no," which meant I was holding a lot of emotions inside. It also meant that that two-letter word would be stuck inside me for two more decades. It took that long for me to finally say the word no; for that one little word to finally leave my face. Once I said it, it felt incredible. I felt so powerful. It was like a new day. A new start. A new beginning.

Later on, I realized that not saying the word "no" was nothing to be ashamed about. During certain times of trauma, your body will take care of you. In that moment, your body is protecting you.

I remember the day I finally said no like it was yesterday. I was already getting med boarded at the time. This meant that I was being evaluated for fitness for duty, both mentally and physically according to Army medical regulations. I decided to go see my provider, whom I'd been seeing for about three years. I started taking care of myself. He mentioned to me how much I had grown and improved. I was talking more, which was helpful for me. He remarked that I didn't really talk much at all at first but that I was starting to open up. As my visit was over, he walked me out into the corridor and gave me a hug. It felt awkward but I obliged.

Several months later, I made an appointment to see him again. I walked in and sat in my usual chair right by the door. He sat in his usual place at his desk, which was only a few feet away. It was a typical setup. But then, out of nowhere, he got up and approached me as I was still sitting in my chair. I remember looking literally at his waistline. He was inches away from my face. "Where's my hug?" he asked. My eyes dropped. I didn't know how to answer that. I searched my brain for the answer and then it hit me. I could just say no. I said, "No, I don't want to do that." And he paused, still looking down at me. A long pause, and then he backed up, ever so slowly. I got up and walked out of the room.

I think he was reassigned soon after that encounter.

Then I did it again. I was on a roll. I had an arsenal at my disposal that I had never used before. This time, as I was going through the med board process, I had to go to the hospital to get some tests done, including an EKG. I arrived at my appointment at my scheduled time and waited for the technician to get there. A tall, overweight male entered the room. I immediately had an uncomfortable feeling. I had had EKGs before and knew they were quite intimate—and here was a male about to do this test for me. I sat on the hospital bed as he proceeded to grab some swabs and some gel substance and turn to me with the items, one in each hand. I asked him, what he was going to do with the items. He said he needed to clean the area. I asked him what area he was referring to, and he said, "the area under your bra line so I can place the electrodes."

I just needed to hear him verbalize what I already assumed. So I asked him if there were any females who do the test. He said no one was available at the moment, so I told him I could wait. I sat there for an hour before a female came in to do the test. Just imagine how many young female soldiers he had done that to.

Compartmentalizing and reframing thoughts

While enduring all this hostility and conflict, I knew that if I was spending time dwelling on negativity, then I wasn't spending time on the positive things I could do for myself in order to help myself. Negativity is a distraction. I knew I needed to get to work. The game was on.

I knew I needed to keep detailed notes about what was happening around me, to plan, and to make contacts. I knew I needed to do research. I couldn't take care of business if I were stuck on one thought or one emotion (negativity). I had to turn those thoughts and emotions off so I could get to work. And that's what I did. For me, analysis was akin to using a flowchart. In my head, I imagined a situation like it was a battlefield, like an overhead projection. I would recognize my starting point and decide what I wanted in the end. Then I'd map out responses and courses of action until I could satisfactorily get to my desired end state. Then I'd go over it again, and again, and again. I would do this until I was satisfied that I could get what I wanted.

Then I'd check it again: trust but verify. Afterward, I did what could be considered an "After Action Review" (AAR) to see if there was anything I could've done to make the outcome even better. If by chance, I didn't get the desired outcome or had a momentary setback, I used this as an opportunity. I looked at that instance as practice, a lesson to be learned, and promised myself I'd be ready the next time. I will not "get got" again. In other words, I took the hit and kept it moving.

To keep on moving, I compartmentalized everything, and I got really good at it. In my mind, I could flip a switch. If I was dealing with something or somebody that was sending negativity my way, I knew I had to turn that off. I knew I needed to take whatever that situation was, put it in a box, deal with it or ignore it, and then close the box. That would be the end of it. If it was someone just saying negative things about me, I could just ignore it because I knew who I was. I knew my worth. I knew I brought value to my unit and my command, so nothing they ever did to me could ever stick.

I also organized my thoughts. I started off being mindful of how I felt before, during, and after certain situations. After doing that enough times, I became disciplined about how I would respond and how I would take care of myself afterward. It was like having a shield or armor. If I had no emotions, I was better able to handle situations. I decided what the end state was that I wanted, and then mapped out different responses to see which one was most likely to get me what I wanted. Then I took action.

I couldn't do that if I was emotional. When you're emotional, you can't think logically, and you make mistakes. This is why emotional control is so important. For a long time emotions were useless to me. They were a distraction that served no purpose. I learned that my first reaction might not be the best, so I trained myself to pause, stop for a moment, and think. "What is it that I want? What am I dealing with? How do I get what I want?" I was able, in real time, to disconnect from the emotion, analyze the situation, then take action.

If you can, take on the mindset that everything is just a game, and you will always be a winner. This takes the emotion out of. It is just a game. Before you start to play, know who you are and what you're made of. I would tell myself all the time, "I'm always a winner. I never lose." This is how I consciously started reframing my thoughts about everything. You don't have to play the game, but you do have to know the rules. If you know the rules, then you can make better decisions. You can define what being a winner means to you.

I also started using imagery to help me reframe my thoughts and get past emotional trauma. I used anything that I found useful: songs, people, public figures, lyrics, stars in the sky, prayers, an oak tree. I started using imagery as a little girl. Anytime I was outside at night or riding in the back of a car, I would look up in the sky and see these three stars in a row. I decided that these three stars were mine and belonged to me. At any time, on any night I could look up and they would be there. It was like having my own guardian angel. Later on as an adult, I decided to research what those stars actually were and they were Orion's Belt.

I used an oak tree as a symbol of motivation because an oak tree cannot be moved. When I was my most productive self, I equated my productivity to being an oak tree. I was upright, strong, and could withstand anything. But there came times when I started leaning on people, but I would sometimes pick the wrong ones. Disappointment, betrayal. . . it was so very stressful and disheartening. I was no longer the mighty oak. My feelings and emotions didn't match with that image I had of myself. That disconnect is what drove me to work to stand upright. I had to build myself back up to where I was.

To reframe my thoughts further, I started identifying with certain heroic, strong, leading characters. I always imagined myself as the hero. I didn't need anyone who looked like me to believe in myself. I was Neo in The Matrix. I was Russell Crowe in Gladiator. I was Meg Ryan in Courage Under Fire. I was Demi Moore in GI Jane. I was Denzel Washington in Crimson Tide.

I used certain people as inspiration. Command Sgt. Maj. Victor Angry, Gen. Colin Powell, Maj. Gen. Timothy McKeithen, and Brig. Gen. Janis Karpinski were people I admired. When things weren't going well for me, I could look at people and not take the adversity or their hostility personally. I would think, "If bad things could happen to these people, then who am I and why would I be special to not go through negativity?" Those thoughts helped me put things into perspective.

| 11 |

Attempting to Survive Fort Bragg

After therapy, I felt recharged. I just needed to last a little bit longer: just long enough until I could leave Fort Bragg. Since I had been away from work for three months, I was allowed to report to work day-on and day-off for a month until I got acclimated back to the work environment. April 21, 2016, was my first day back at work. On my work days, I managed to have responsibilities that didn't require going into my office at Fort Bragg. Five days later, on April 26, I took care of some PC business at the Soldier Support Center at Fort Bragg since I had my PCS orders, but on April 28, I had no other business to take care of. Since it was a work day, I needed to go in, but I was terrified of seeing Sgt. Maj. Vinker.

I never left home. I had panicked before but somehow always managed to build myself up enough to go back into the fight. I could put on my armor, which was my uniform, and battle once more, but this time was different. I was getting ready for work as usual, but the panic got more and more intense as the minutes went on. I kept imagining that I had to see Sgt. Maj. Vinker. Once I decided to stay home, I felt a sense of relief. No one called me, sent me a text message, or knocked on my door during the period they were "looking for me." Hours later, after 6 p.m., my boss 1st Sgt. Orgain called me on my cell phone and asked me where I was on April 26 and 28, 2016. I told him that on April 26 I went to the Soldier Support Center and on April 28 I had panicked and never left home. It was a short conversation, and that was it. My Commander said he had called the military police (MP) and hospitals, but he did not call me. Both days, I never left the base, and one of those days I never left my room. Little did I know that he was about to charge me for being absent without leave (AWOL) and that was why he had waited to call me until 6 p.m., as a certain amount of time had to elapse before they could consider a soldier AWOL.

I had no idea what this process meant as I had never experienced it before, but I soon found out that they had to read the Article 15 to me and give me a certain amount of time to speak to legal assistance.

My commander at the time was Maj. Dumley Shallo, an SF soldier. Maj. Shallo said, "Master Sgt. Watkins you will sign this document today?" I had no idea what this meant and didn't know there was anything I wasn't supposed to sign.

Maj. Shallo directed me to initial the block for my choice of taking the Article 15 or the court-martial. I told him I didn't know the benefits of selecting either one, so he explained it to me. I selected the Article 15 because, as Maj. Shallo explained it, I could be convicted at a court-martial. In essence, I would be rolling the dice. I knew he was setting me up. I knew none of this was fair, but I had no idea how much power he had in controlling the outcome of a court-martial. So I took my chances with something that would be done and over with, as opposed to a drawn out and unfair trial. According to him, it would remain local. I could still PCS to NGB and get beyond all of this conflict. Did I believe him? No. I weighed my options, made a decision, and hoped for the best outcome possible.

Soon thereafter, I was told that an investigating officer (IO) was coming to meet with me. I thought I was finally getting some relief and my complaints about the hostile work environment were being heard. I found out later it was a fake investigation. Lt. Swinson was the IO assigned to my case, but he took the information I told him and relayed it to Maj. Shallo and Sgt. Maj. Vinker. Not only that, but he also lied about what I told him and got the soldiers in my section to write statements against me, including my E7, the same SFC I had mentored into the confident person she was. I felt so betrayed. But what I learned from that was not only to watch who I talked to but to also understand that these guys are not just in the Army of One. The males I worked with were not just in the National Guard. They all had "long tabs." They were all Green Berets, which was something we would never have in common. I would never be in that group, that circle. They stuck together because I was an outsider.

After that, I was told to report to Maj. Shallo's office. There were three others there including my boss at the time Sgt. Maj. Shanequa Jackson. She was useless. I felt like it was me against all of them. They informed me they were going to read the Article 15 and formally accuse me of going AWOL. After 27 years of immaculate service, this is what they did to me— and on my birthday.

According to the Article 15, I didn't report for work at HHC, the headquarters company; however, I never worked at HHC. My place of duty was at 4th BN, USAJFKSWCS.

I called my therapist to write a statement on my behalf, which she did.

Then, I called the Ms. Chardonnay Johnson, ombudsman at Womack, just before I saw an attorney for the second time at Trial Defense Service and asked for her help in dealing with this Article 15 second reading, which was due to occur in a couple of hours. She didn't understand why no one who was in a place to do something did anything. She was useless as well.

I was able to see another lawyer because I was still seriously contemplating taking the court-martial. It was about two hours before the second reading that I finally had a better understanding of what was about to take place. I decided to take the court-martial, felt good about taking the court-martial, and I had no qualms about remaining on Fort Bragg to defend myself.

While sitting in the parking lot at Bryant Hall, I asked Lt. Swinson if he could print the statement from my therapist for me, which he did after I emailed it to him.

Command Sgt. Maj. Mitchell, the 4th Battalion Sergeant Major, had privately told me that "everything was going to be OK" and that I didn't have to take the court-martial, which I was definitely going to do. I was distraught, angry, frustrated, confused, anxious, and afraid the entire time.

Maj. Shallo had repeated several times that all of this was going to go away after I left his office. But, if it was all going away, why did we continue to go through the process? It made no sense.

Maj. Shallo had all of the Article 15 documents laid out on his desk. Once I told him where I was on April 26, 2016, he explicitly said, "That's not what Lt. Swinson said." While deceptively opening a top drawer of his desk, he pulled out what he indicated was 1st Lt. Swinson's statement. I was confused about this because Lt. Swinson told me he was investigating my complaints of a hostile work environment. This is when I learned he was actually investigating me and chose to lie about me. I rebutted everything in Lt. Swinson's statement and, just like that, Maj. Shallo returned the document to the same drawer in his desk.

I presented documents on my own behalf. But I accidentally mixed up the dates by referring to April 21 instead of April 26. Because of this mix-up, I was charged with lying.

After speaking with Maj. Shallo, I asked the paralegal, SFC Stanford for a copy of the Article 15 packet. As soon as I got my hands on the packet, I went straight to then Lt. Swinson's statement. This was the first time I was able to read it. Once I read it, it was clear why Maj. Shallo set Lt. Swinson's statement aside and didn't read it nor allow me to read it. Lt. Swinson failed to mention in his statement that I told him where I was on April 26 and 28, 2016. In his statement, portraying himself as an investigator on my behalf and that of my ARNG coworkers, he made it seem as if I was AWOL for no reason instead of swearing to what I actually told him. As soon as I left the office I went to my car and recorded a video of what happened. I was going to fight it because nothing that they did was fair. I didn't deserve an Article 15 and I felt that they conspired to set me up.

They wanted to keep the Article 15 a secret, but I said, "No, I'm telling everybody." It turns out that being a Master Sergeant/E-8 receiving an Article 15 meant there was a certain process that was supposed to be followed. The Article 15 was supposed to be reviewed by the base Commander, but I did not know this at the time. Maybe that was why he wanted to keep it a secret.

From panic attacks to promotion

Since that incident in May 2016, I'd been able to make it to work, but on June 3, I was driving on base and panic came up out of nowhere. Suddenly, I didn't know what to do. I tried to think of someplace I could go to get help. I literally had no idea what to do or where to go. I thought the safest place for me to go would be the base hospital. So I drove there, but then what? Did I have an emergency? Did I really want to potentially sit in the emergency room for hours over nothing?

I decided I'd just find a place to park so I could figure things out. I needed time to think, but I needed to let someone know where I was, so I sent a message to 1st Sgt. Orgain. I told him where I was and that I didn't know what to do. He thought I was joking and was no help at all. I ended up calling the Veterans Crisis Line. I just needed someone to talk to. They helped me figure out what to do next. I was not injured or in danger, so I eventually just went home.

Three days later, on June 6, I made it to work but I only got as far as the parking lot. I could not bring myself to get out of my car. Usually, if I was having trouble, I could sit in my car in the parking lot for fifteen to thirty minutes and convince myself to go in. But on that day, I couldn't get out of my car. I was that afraid to even go into the building.

That building represented the embodiment of evil. I started to panic, so I called the Veterans Crisis Line again. It wasn't enough. Then I got "broke faced." I had wet stuff pouring from my eyes. My phone rang. It was my boss. "Where are you?" he asked. I replied, "I'm in the parking lot." I was a mess. They ended up sending another Soldier out to the parking lot to get me. He drove around the parking lot until he spotted my vehicle. . . only I wouldn't go in. They ended up assigning me to a different office.

One day, I had to report to Maj. Shallo's office to discuss my outgoing plan for the PCS orders I'd received in April to move back to NGB. As I was sitting there across from him, I started to glance out the window. He was talking but I wasn't listening. I wanted him to stop talking so I could leave the room, but he kept talking. My anger was so intense that it started to show on my face. I was furious because I knew he was trying to prevent me from leaving Fort Bragg. Broken as my face was and leaking like a sieve, I looked out into the courtyard and imagined myself there. I couldn't leave the room, but I imagined it. What could I do to escape? I visualized myself going through the window. I thought that if I used enough force, I could make it. Relief was just beyond my reach. I was trapped in a room I couldn't escape from. Thinking back, I wonder how prisoners of war feel.

After that was over, they still weren't done. I had to repeatedly go back to the Commander's office to speak to him about something or other. They were really wearing me down, so much so that my face was leaking every time. I was embarassed at first, but then I decided to reframe my thoughts. I accepted that this was going to be difficult. I accepted that I was going to be broke faced walking through the Orderly Room in front of all those males. But this did not mean I was weak. If anyone thought so, they would be sorely disappointed. I decided that I was going to be strong internally and get through it. As a senior NCO, a Master Sergeant with over 27 years of active duty, I needed to show those soldiers that I had courage and that if you stand up for what you believe in, you can make it to the other side. I was going to show them what that looked like in real time.

I had other panic attacks. I went to a dance event in Virginia. While there, I went to a shopping center not far from the hotel but I couldn't find my car when I came out of the store. I immediately thought it was stolen and started mapping out next steps (call police, call insurance). But then I saw it. As soon as I got in my car, the panic hit. It just came out of nowhere. Then I remembered the grounding technique from IOP. I started naming things around me, and it worked. I panicked again on the way to the ballroom, and I panicked in the ballroom. I panicked going through airport security. I panicked in large crowds or when there were changes to a routine. But I knew I had to fix it. The solution was out there, I just had to find it.

Maj Shallo tried to extend my time at Fort Bragg for another six months so they could "take care of me," but my orders were to go back to NGB that same year. Since Maj. Shallo was active duty, he had no clue how National Guard orders worked, but I did. (That was the office at NGB I had just left, and I trained the Soldier who replaced me.) I called that soldier and told him the Commander was trying to extend me for six months, but I didn't need that long to clear and process out.

I was trying to leave Fort Bragg as soon as possible. I called my replacement and told him, "Nope." I only need thirty days. I had submitted a promotion packet. I was going to get that promotion. After all, I was already one of the top E8s in my field. I was at the top of the Order of Merit List of all E8s in the Title 10 AGR program. For the first time my goal was to be the first female First Sergeant of the NGB installation. I just needed thirty days. Sure getting charged with AWOL was pretty bad, but because I had worked for the promotion board, I knew being labeled AWOL has no bearing on the process. Not getting a promotion recommendation from the first O6 in my Chain of Command was pretty bad as well. But having my Commander hand-carry the promotion list to me with my name on it was PRICELESS!

They didn't know what I knew. They didn't know who I knew. I was able to get through the Sergeant Major/E9 promotion board that year because I never let them know what I was up to. I just did it.

The harassment didn't stop

Later on, I ran into my E7 in the PX. Her daughters, who loved me, were there and saw me, "Ms. Erinn!" they shouted. I walked them back over to where their mother was, and she started talking to me as if nothing were new. But I asked her, "Why did you do it?" I had taken such good care of her. I let her leave when she wanted in order to take care of her girls. She had time off when she needed to. I trained her to stick up for herself. I didn't understand it. Her response was, "I didn't know." Well she could've told me that that's what they did instead of letting me find out by reading her name on a statement she wrote against me.

Since I was working in a separate building, the Maj. Shallo and 1st Sgt. Orgain decided to pay me a visit. This building had its own conference room. So before I went in there, I grabbed my phone, put it on record, stuck it in my pocket and waited at the position of parade rest. Maj. Shallo and 1st Sgt Orgain walked in and started lodging complaints against me. Nothing they were saying made any sense. Maj. Shallo was doing most of the talking. He was saying things that were provably untrue. He was lying about me to my face. I knew this because I knew details and he didn't. In my spare time, I had this calendar I kept and I would review it periodically throughout the day every day. So I knew details like the back of my hand. I kept my same calm tone of voice, "No sir, that's not true." I kept saying, "No sir." and "No sir, that's not what happened." Next thing I know, 1st Sgt. Orgain walks up to me, inches from my face. I thought to myself, "What in the entire hell do you think you're doing?" But the words wouldn't leave my face. I just stood there. I stood my ground. In my mind I was thinking, "It's your move 1st Sergeant. What are you going to do?" Moments later, he stepped back. HE moved. Not me. What in the entire hell did he think he was doing? We are the SAME grade. The only thing that separates us is your diamond. 1st Sergeant, you are a nobody. You don't scare me.

I decided to use the open-door policy to see the SWCS Battalion Commander. When I arrived, he had a female on standby to be present during our meeting. She and I were sitting at a table across from his desk. By the time I had gotten my point across he ended up bragging to me about how much he had done to reduce sexual harassment in the military. He showed me his binder of the work he had accomplished. I was not impressed. I told him, "Sir, do you realize that the same people keep going to these sexual harassment briefings all the time?" My face started leaking again. He even shared with me that some Battalion Commander and his son were going around breaking into people's homes in his neighborhood on base. I have no idea why he shared this with me. Even as we were done and I turned to walk out of his office, he still had something to say. So I paused, listened, then I walked out the door.

Others recognized my achievements

While many leaders tried to tear me down, many others recognized my achievements. As an E8, I was one of the senior ranking NCOs in my unit. This was around the time that they were about to start allowing females to come to Special Forces School. The Battalion Commander at the Special Forces School asked me if I would be an observer for the females who were coming to SF training. For him to ask me to do this, I had to be doing something right, and he noticed.

I knew it was a great opportunity. I just didn't realize how big it was at the time because it was my nature to handle any task that came my way. Also, the hostility in my unit was still going on, and I saw taking this new opportunity as a way to escape the hostile working environment I was in. But the idea that this Lieutenant Colonel, this white SF Lieutenant Colonel, came and directly asked me to do this left a huge impression on me.

This is something I sometimes forget but that gives me validation that I was a good person, a good soldier, respected, and well-liked. You have to have these qualities and more in order to be asked by this Commander to fill that position. It was an honor and a privilege.

This Lieutenant Colonel saw within me someone who was equipped to handle this new job. Looking back, a lot of things I've accomplished make me question the entire arguments of systemic racism and sexism. I never needed to beat anyone over the head. I never needed to force the issue. I always knew I just needed to do my job, do it well, and let the chips fall where they may.

The end of my career

When it was all said and done, however, I never sealed the deal because the conflict surrounding me was so massive. It was up to me to make it happen. At the time, I was so focused on battling my boss that I lost sight of that opportunity. All that I had done and accomplished was not enough. Fort Bragg was the most difficult challenge that I had ever dealt with to date. It was like I had been in training for my entire career in order to deal with what I experienced at Fort Bragg. Even though I was always two steps ahead of the conspiracy to discredit and humiliate me, and even though I had contacts and employed strategies to prevent that from happening, it just wasn't enough in the end.

I learned that one of the SF Soldiers who used to come and talk to me had a brain injury. I didn't think he was actually working, but I knew that his Command was letting him take care of himself. And that worked. I was having some challenges as well and decided to advocate for myself. I had been fighting for so long that I was mentally worn out. I decided to ask my my new Company Commander, Maj. Richard Loman, if I could have time to take care of myself just as had been done before. I didn't mention who. We were standing outside at the time and I was at the position of attention. He wasn't telling me what I wanted to hear so I decided that I didn't want to listen to his voice anymore, and I tuned him out. Then it started sprinkling. As the rain started coming, he asked if I wanted to go inside. "No, sir." Then my face started leaking. People were walking by. I didn't care. I just wanted him to stop talking, so I could salute him and leave. Then it happened. I don't know why I did it, but I gradually, centimeter by centimeter, started turning my position away from him. In my head, I had already dismissed him. I was just waiting for him to shut up so I could go. But I kept inching and turning away from him ever so slowly, until it was undeniable that I was no longer facing him. I was actually at an angle. Then it happened. Instead of him saying, "Master. Sgt. Watkins, what are you doing?" or giving me a direct order to face him, HE moved to face me. At that very moment, I felt so powerful. I made him move. I did that. He finally told me what I wanted to hear. "Master Sgt. Watkins, go home and take care of yourself."

From that moment on, I never had to work there again. My only requirement was to check in with an SF E7 who worked in the Orderly Room. That was fine by me.

I already had orders to PCS to NGB, so I thought it was all over and I could leave Fort Bragg. What could possibly stop me now? It seems they still had one more trick up their sleeve. They put me on a P3 profile for mental health reasons. The Army has a system of classifying individuals according to their functional abilities. The factors considered are physical capacity or stamina, upper extremities, lower extremities, hearing and ears, eyes, and psychiatric. P1 and P2 profiles are temporary. P3 is a permanent profile that prevents soldiers from PCSing until the profiling issue is resolved. With a P3 profile, I could not leave Fort Bragg. Maj. Loman referred me to the Medical Treatment Facility (MTF) for evaluation. This evaluation resulted in a Medical Evaluation Board that then referred me to a Physical Evaluation Board. All of this meant that I was found unfit to continue serving in the military. That's how they did it. I was medically retired, but at least, because I had over twenty years of active duty, I received my full retirement.

| 12 |

Post-Military Life

During this time, I didn't really trust or like people. I didn't enjoy being around them. The only person I trusted was myself, and I was suspicious of happy people. I thought to myself, "What the hell are you so happy about?" If I passed someone on the street and they looked at me, I thought, "What the hell are you looking at?" I mentioned this to the group when I was still in IOP therapy. I noticed the thing.

So, in order to get past that negativity, I relied on something I had used before: facts and data. I paid attention to trends and tendencies. Instead of using them to decide who was out to get me, I used them to prove that people aren't out to get me.

Is this person bothering me? Did this person hurt me in any way?

I used questions and answers to build up my facts, data, trends, and tendencies. The answer to my questions was consistently, "no." I determined that people were not concerned about me. They were too busy going about their daily lives. And if they looked at me, so what? Maybe they were just being friendly.

Reflecting on my career

When I was at NGB, I purchased this book called *48 Laws of Power*. As I started reading it, I never got past the first rule: "Never outshine the master." That is so true. That was what my problem was, if you can look at it like that. I don't think I ever tried to be better than or outshine my leaders. I always wanted to make them shine and make them look good because when they looked good, then the rest of us did too. But it was never enough. I still wound up outshining many of my leaders, particularly the ones who were against me.

At one time, I was told that I was a threat to them. I wasn't even trying to be a threat; I wasn't even my best self yet. I was always trying to get there. I may have done what appeared to be remarkable things but to me they weren't so remarkable at all. I was just being myself trying to be my best soldier self. But I guess trying to get to my best self was threatening. They bullied me and shut me down in a number of ways, trying to get me to comply with mediocrity and become a "team player" (a.k.a. not better than them).

At the end of my career I finally learned that it was okay to take credit for myself. I had to learn that it was okay to be "selfish." By being selfish, I mean being my best self despite the threat others felt; I mean taking care of myself. From the moment I decided to put myself first, there was never anything that anyone could hold over my head to make me comply. I would no longer require their approval to be my best self. It was as if I flipped the switch and a lightbulb came on one day: not being my best self only hurts me.

Getting there was always a work in progress, though. Any progress in life is a journey. It's not a straight line. You have good days as well as bad days. When I have bad days now, what makes a difference is that I know what I can do. It's hard to take my own advice, but I've practiced (and still practice) doing the things that I need to do and things I want to do. It's called practice because it doesn't come naturally. But when you practice consistently, it gets easier each time until it becomes second nature.

I got better doing these things as I learned more about myself. I looked up the meaning of my name which perfectly explained the kind of person I am:

"You are gifted with natural leadership and the capacity to accumulate great wealth!

"Your path will lead you to work out the difference between money and the true value of life.

"You have great talent for management, and you understand the material world.

"You intuitively know what makes virtually any enterprise work, and you always look at the greater vision.

"You are born to be in charge and be a visionary! Power and authority come naturally to you although you will also learn that it is lonely at the top.

"You will be successful in any field where you can be the executive decision-maker, especially in business and financial matters."

Everything in my life's story supports this description. In group therapy, we learned about spirit animals. I thought mine would be a white tiger, but it's actually an owl.

An owl symbolizes intuition, transition, wisdom, silence, observation, quick wit, independence, power, intelligence, and protection. Its ability to see in the dark endows it with the energies of the moon and night, as well as makes it symbolic of mystery, hidden knowledge, and feminine fertility. To have an owl as your totem animal means that you are strong-willed, perceptive, and a great empathizer.

Having sound intuitive abilities, you are quick to discern the real intentions behind other's actions or motives. Thus, people cannot deceive you on any occasion. You are also adaptable and face different situations of life with an easy-going manner.

After all of the time I spent in the military, getting better at being my best self, I'm in such a better place. I can look back now and acknowledge that. As I was going through it, I used resilience, which I didn't know was resilience at the time, in order to keep myself as healthy as possible so I could deal with the stressors and trauma. I needed my body to take care of me. I was in hostile work environments repeatedly and constant conflict. I was always in survival mode. I used emotional control to help make rational decisions in times of tremendous stress. These were skills I was building, but I still needed some work.

I learned to control automatic thoughts by programming my own thoughts to handle certain situations. I chose them based on which one would give me the best outcome and allow me to get what I want.

I had to learn that some people come into your life for a specific purpose. Once that purpose is done, good or bad, it's time to let them go. They've performed their function and it's time to move on.

Gratitude became an important practice in my recovery. I'm grateful for the little things because it could always be worse. At least I'm not cold. I'm not hot. I have a place to sleep. I have food to eat. Suddenly things aren't so bad after all.

Even though I got through it and was still successful, I ended up being diagnosed with major depressive disorder, PTSD, and anxiety.

I still have my struggles, and I do use some of the same coping strategies today.

My sister has consistently marveled at how I got through everything. She told me that through it all, I always knew what to do. I always had a plan. She said that whenever I called her to talk about what was going on, she waited for me to ask her for help. But I never did. I never had to. She said, "You always had it figured out. You had solutions for everything. You had a plan for everything. If they said this, you were going to do that. And if they said that, you were going to do this."

My goal now is to show people how I did it. It was difficult but not impossible. Some things were simple but not easy. Anyone can do it with the right amount of willpower and determination. And I want to share that. I've never been one to keep good information to myself. I've always wanted my leaders to use me for what I know. I'm here to be helpful. And for my soldiers and colleagues, if you ask me a question, I'm not only going to give you the answer, but I'm also going to show you where I got it so the next time you can find it yourself. I want you to be the next to take over when I'm gone.

When I look back on my military career, the one lesson that sticks out to me is that you can always find a way forward. There is always a way to get unstuck. You're never permanently stuck. There are always options. You have to have faith that the answers are out there. When you feel stuck, it's only because you haven't figured it out yet. And asking for help is an option. Someone out there has the answer, and you just have to find them. Look for the light at the end of the tunnel because it's there. You just have to see it. If you haven't called every number in your contacts and every number in the phone book, then you're not done. It's not over. You have to keep pushing. If you got through today, then you can do it again, one more time. Sometimes you have to take a break, back up, and regroup. But that's okay. It's okay to feel sorrow and pity. Take time for sorrow. Take as much time as you need. Then get back in the fight. Keep adding on and keep building. Step by step, one at a time. Keep making progress, little by little, until you get what you want, your desired end state.

I beat depression once again

In 2020, after a three-year break, I moved to Tennessee to live with my sister. Later that same year around Christmas, I had stopped driving. I stopped leaving home. I got through the day by watching TV, all day until it was time to go to sleep. But midnight came and I wasn't sleepy. I was wide awake. I was starting to be afraid to go to sleep because I didn't know how I was going to get through the night. I thought I could fix everything, but this was something I had trouble with. I would sleep for one, maybe two hours at a time and then wake up. I ballooned to 185 lbs., but something started changing.

In my mind I knew I wanted to change but I wasn't quite there yet. Whenever I got discouraged, I looked for things that showed progress. I made sure that I kept actionable items: things I could do. That was important to me because I didn't want to be idle. I didn't want to be doing nothing. I didn't want to be sitting around and waiting. I was always asking, "What else can I do? What's the next thing?" I always stayed busy.

My first step was to change my diet. I had lost 30 lbs. twice one year just by changing my diet so I knew it could be done. If I did it before, I could do it again. . . another strategy. I started walking around the block but I always felt vulnerable to "attack," some imaginary enemy that I had to watch out for, so I wasn't consistent. Since I liked to dance, I started looking for dance classes in Nashville. I had a counselor at the time whom I spoke to weekly and she suggested that I look for dance videos online and maybe try some steps. I found one, and then a week later I tried again and found another. I also went to my own YouTube channel and reminisced about the dances I already knew. I tried them out to see if I could remember the steps. Ultimately, I came across a line dance class, but it was clear across town. Driving had been out of the question, but I knew that if I wanted to get to where the magic was, I needed to get outside of my comfort zone. I was going to reclaim what was mine.

So that's what I did. I took a deep breath, got in my car, and started driving. I had my music playing, and I was focused on my destination. It was a good thing I went to that class at that time because two friends of mine whom I hadn't seen in years, one who lived on the east coast, were there. I was so happy and they were so glad to see me. They gave me the biggest hugs. It was amazing! If I hadn't gone, I would've missed out on all that magic.

Since I was eating better, I knew that I needed to start moving in order to lose the extra weight. So I decided to go back to the class one more time. The first one was Monday and the second one was Wednesday. I decided that I liked the class so, one day at a time, I went back again and again. Now I'm an official instructor for the class, and I've been going twice a week, every week.

During this time of not driving myself, my sister was taking me where I needed to go, we would pass by a golf course near where we lived. I decided that, since I had acquired some donated golf clubs, I wanted to look and act like a retiree. Every time I passed this golf course, I kept deciding that that's what I wanted to do. Two years later, since I was now driving myself to the store and to the gym, I decided that I would go there and just check it out. I'd do a "drive-by." Don't think about it; just do it. I was wearing my Army Veteran hat when I went into the golf shop. The man behind the counter told me they had a ladies clinic that met every Thursday. He also told me about this program coming up called PGA Hope, a six-week program that teaches veterans how to play golf using professional golfers. I was golfing twice a week on Wednesdays and Thursdays for six weeks straight. I also gained some friends whom I also golfed with.

So how in the world do I keep doing this? I decided a long time ago that I needed to go where the magic is. I couldn't get there by staying in my comfort zone. In 2014, I noticed something I wanted to do: Tough Mudder. Even though I decided to do it, I wasn't convinced that I would. But what I could do was just go there and see what it looked like. The drive-by. I got to the location and started walking toward the festivities, and people were passing me covered in mud. No worries. I looked around and decided that I could at least sign up since I'd driven all that way. I went to the check in tent and signed up, which felt really good. I got a bag, T-shirt, and headband. At least I did that much. I looked around again and saw a group of people standing around and I thought, "Let me see what they're doing." By that point, I was still not convinced that I was even going to participate, but at least I was there.

I put my bag down and discovered that those people were standing around waiting to start. There were different groups that started at different times. I saw the starting point, so I went with them. At least I could do that much. Next thing I knew, I was over the first obstacle and on my way. Someone behind me said, "Hey are you by yourself?" I was. She offered for me to join her and her three friends, so I did.

There were lots of obstacles but the most memorable one was called "Walk the Plank." I'm not a swimmer and, since I didn't have to do every obstacle, I figured I'd skip that one and let my new friends have all the fun. I was standing next to one of the workers and told him I couldn't swim. He said some guy jumped earlier and couldn't swim. "Really? Hold my stuff!" He said they let that person jump as a solo jumper. There was a diver already in the "water." I decided to do it and I asked him to record it for me.

I climbed the ladder, pointed to the diver, and said, "I know where you work. I will find you!" Midair, I decided to hold my nose and I hit the water. Since I hadn't ever jumped in deep water before I had no idea what to expect, but I had seen divers on TV, and they kicked their feet, so I started kicking my feet. I noticed I was running out of air and wasn't getting to the surface fast enough, so I decided to start using my arms. Then I felt the diver grab me and pull me up. When I came to the surface everyone was cheering my name. It was amazing. My friends said I was down there for a while. But now I had bragging rights!

Using the coping techniques I'd learned, I was able to get through every obstacle of the twelve-mile race. I remember this story any time I feel apprehensive about something I want to do. I remember Walk the Plank, and I take a deep breath and just dive in. Because that's where the magic is. Whether it's deciding to go for a walk when all I can do at the time is sit on the porch. If I can do that, I can walk to the street. Then I can walk to the corner. If I can do that, what else can I do? I can take a deep breath and walk around the block.

Finding my people

Throughout all of this time, I made it my goal to never be the smartest one in the room. I gravitated toward people who would challenge my intelligence. I surrounded myself with people who wanted to see me succeed instead of those who want to see me fail. I highly encourage people to do this. One benefit to that approach was that I found mentors. Mentorship was important to me. Mentorship can come from multiple sources. There were people who crossed my path who gave me mentorship but didn't really realize it. It was a little thing here and a little thing there that I got from one person or another, that I added to my toolbox. I also had opportunities to mentor others.

Sometimes, I come across people when I'm out and about town or when I'm online who I think I could help, based on what they share with me. I can tell if they're ready to receive the information I have because not everyone is ready or willing to deal with their problems head on like I have learned. I'm grateful to be able to do that.

It's also important to find and connect with like-minded people. After I got out of the military, I found other veterans to connect with. When you do this, you can compare and contrast your experiences because we all have similar stories. You need to be around people who think like you do and have gone through the things you have. Everyone wants to be surrounded by people who understand them. You're no different.

After I retired, I joined the Fayetteville American Legion at Post 202. After only six months, I was asked to run for the position of Adjutant. I ran for the position and was elected. It was the male members who asked me to run because they thought I could do something to help the Post.

The annual convention was coming up so I decided I would go and learn more about the American Legion as a whole. We could attend any meetings we wanted to, so I specifically sought out the ones where the leadership was. The gentleman next to me graciously pointed out to me who was who. After the meeting, I went up to one of the leaders and introduced myself. I just wanted to say hello.

Later on, they asked for volunteers to participate in the American Legion's new ad campaign. I thought to myself, "Sure why not?" We all met in the auditorium and took pictures. Some people had lines to say. Then someone got my attention and asked if I minded if my photo was taken. Sure, why not? What I didn't know is that that photo would end up on the cover of the national magazine. You know what that meant? ALL the people whom I used to work with, who caused me so much grief and mental anguish, who happened to be members of the American Legion, would see my face once again. I'm a winner!

As I meet and talk to people, I see that they are going through some of the things that I've gone through. I've already addressed a lot of the issues they're dealing with and I'm in the next phase now. So I see where they are. I understand it; I've been there, so I'm grateful that I went through it. Gratitude is key to being your best self. Being grateful means that you have the emotional control, mind space, and time to reflect on the bright spots here and there in what seemed like years of one long holding pattern. I'm able to see clearly what I wasn't always able to see when I was going through it. I've reclaimed what was mine.

EPILOGUE

My Retirement Ceremony

It was a Thursday and the final day of a veteran women's retreat in Destin, Florida. That evening, we were going to have a sit-down dinner as an end to the event. I thought about going out with the other ladies before dinner, but I took a nap. After waking, I came downstairs and noticed that Sarah was decorating the living room.

"How nice to decorate for our final dinner," I thought. She was decorating with black and gold, Army colors, even though the ladies at the retreat were from different branches. I assumed that the black and gold represented the organization sponsoring the event (Waypoint Vets). I thought about helping out, but we were all shooed away. We were there for relaxation and enjoyment only.

I sat out by the pool for a little while, then I went back upstairs right before it was time for dinner. For some reason, I was running behind everyone else and hurried as best I could to meet up with everyone in the dining area. As I came downstairs, one of the women told me that I needed to grab my journal and a pen (we were given these earlier in the week), so I went back up to my room.

On my way back down, I met another woman in the hallway, so we took the elevator down together. As soon as we made it to the room where we were having dinner, I noticed that all of the women were standing in a group to my left. I didn't notice that they were in formation until I heard the words, "Attention to orders!" I immediately snapped to attention as we're supposed to do.

What followed next was a shock. My "retirement orders" were read by one of the women who was an Army officer. I stood there in shock, not knowing what to think. Another veteran presented me with a cake with my name on it. As I took it, I couldn't talk. Someone took the cake from me, walked me over to the counter, and that's when I saw it. My very own shadow box.

In it was a flag, and on it was a nameplate with my name, MSG ERINN WATKINS, embossed and spelled correctly. It had my dates of service (which were all accurate). How did they know? How did they do this? I had no idea whatsoever that they were considering doing this. It was a total secret to me.

I was reminded of the first day of the retreat when we all took turns introducing ourselves. I was sitting on the corner of the sofa, trying to think of what I was going to say. I had a few things I wanted to mention and then that would be it. Or so I thought.

Several of the female veterans went before me. And as each spoke, the more uncomfortable I got. I was doing everything I could to maintain control. I finally got up and went to the restroom to clear my face. When I came back, I sat down and said nothing. What I had planned to say didn't happen. It didn't work for me. I was so anxious, and it was all so overwhelming. Why?

It was probably because I didn't want to talk too much or take up too much time. But then it all just came out. I wanted them to know how difficult my time in the military was for me and how it was so important for me to control my emotions. I talked about how some situations I had endured in the military had been so hostile, yet I had still managed to show my own individual power. I was still powerful despite what they were doing to me.

I told them that I was very good at my job. I was extremely good at my job no matter where I went. But even at my final duty station, the people with whom I served could not stand me. They hated me so much that they wouldn't give me what I deserved as a Master Sergeant with over twenty-eight years of active duty. They gave me nothing. That's when I told them about how all I received was a flag in a box.

But here I was, over five years later. After all of that waiting, I finally got what I wanted, which was to be surrounded by people who genuinely cared for me. I had been carrying that burden of disgust and humiliation for so long, but now I had an opportunity at a new beginning. All of the anger and anxiety seemed to vanish.

They gave me my retirement ceremony. I no longer have to carry that burden anymore of being owed something I never received because I got something that was meaningful and from the heart of people who genuinely cared about me. Sometimes, the thought of my final day in service rears its ugly head, and the old emotions rise up as well. But I don't let them stay. Through the actions of the women of Waypoint Veterans, I'm reminded of who I really am. I am MSG Erinn Watkins. Army Veteran. Airborne. Pathfinder.

ACKNOWLEDGEMENTS

I would like to express my thanks and gratitude to the people who have supported me, my career, and my goals at some point along the way.

To CSM Victor Angry. US Army Retired: MG Timothy McKeithen. US Army Retired: Mr. Eric Scott and Ms. Yvonne Gines: CSM Perlisa D. Wilson: LTC Steve Morgan: Angela Martin. US Army Retired: SGM Keith Morgan. US Army Retired: MAJ Lee M. Sharber (1970 – 2014). US Army: Kenneth Johnson. US Army Retired: Sarah Lee. CEO Waypoint, US Army Veteran; Kia Kelliebrew; Earin and Ke'Anna Rose.

To the people at JFHQ NJ: that *Certificate of Appreciation* meant so very much to me.

To the LTC at NGB who taught me that my success is not only mine, but that it also needs to be shared.

To the MAJ who walked by me one day and told me to "stay plugged in."

To the leaders at NGB who put me at the top of the E-8 *Order of Merit* list.

To the female Soldier who asked me to be her mentor. I'm so sorry that I let you down. I realize now that I did not have enough within me to share.

To the Special Forces Commander who asked me to be an observer for future SF female students.

To the Special Forces MAJ who mentally helped me get through the longest counseling session ever.

To those who helped me get through the medical board process. It was stress-free and what started me on my journey to healing and recovery.

To all the people who were on my team and didn't know it.

BIOGRAPHY
MSG Erinn Watkins, Army (Ret.)

Master Sergeant (MSG) Erinn Watkins is an accomplished Army Veteran with an impressive military resume spanning nearly 30 years. She was one of the first women to become an Army Pathfinder, she helped test and develop important military equipment and programs, and she turned around on the ladder to success to help mentor younger Soldiers on the same path. Now retired, Erinn is proud to be a Pathfinder in a new way – she's reclaimed her power after a turbulent career and leaned into a new mission: showing others how she survived it all.

"Throughout my military career I dealt with a lot of hostility and conflict. I dealt with a lot of toxic people and despite this, I was still very successful. My last few years in the military were ... the most mentally challenging thing I had ever experienced. But using my previous experiences, I managed to come out on top. I want to show people how I did this."

Adding "Author" to an already-impressive resume, Erinn's new book *PathfYnder* takes readers on an illuminating and empowering journey to finding their best selves. Leveraging her own experiences – no story is off limits – Erinn lays the path to navigating hostile work environments, toxic leadership, and more.

Erinn has been showing people the best path to success nearly her entire life. Away from the Army, Erinn is a well-known dance instructor (@PetitePrincess92 on YouTube), teaching styles like Soul Line Dance, Chicago Steppin', and more. Her signature style of instruction helps students to learn quickly while still having a great time.

As a 100% disabled Veteran, Erinn spends her time giving back. She joined the American Legion in 2017, served as the Adjutant of Post 202 in North Carolina, and was on the cover of the Legion Magazine in 2018. Most recently, she's now a Veteran Mentor for the local Veterans Treatment Court.

Erinn has one son, a graduate of Embry Riddle Aeronautical University. She currently resides in Nashville, Tennessee.

A HISTORY OF SUCCESS

MY ACCOMPLISHMENTS
MSG ERINN WATKINS, US ARMY RETIRED
JOINED: 1988, RETIRED: 2017

Military Accomplishments

- **Last assignment:**
  National Guard Liaison, August 2012 - Aug 2017
  US Army John F Kennedy Special Warfare Center and School,
  Ft Bragg, NC

- **Previous Assignments - Enlisted:**
  Army Reserves, New Orleans, LA
  Army National Guard (ARNG), Nashville, TN
  Army National Guard (ARNG), Ft Dix, NJ
  Army National Guard (ARNG), Baltimore, MD
  Title 32 AGR: TN ARNG, NJ ARNG
  Title 10 AGR: MD ARNG

- **Previous Assignments - Warrant Officer:**
  Regular Army/US Army Reserve, Aviation

Significant Achievements/Events

- Completed Army Pathfinder School in June 1995
- Earned five foreign parachutist badges:

  - Chilean Parachutist Badge
  - Honduran Military Airborne Badge
  - French Army Parachutist Badge
  - German Armed Forces Parachutist Badge
  - Royal Netherlands Parachute Badge

- Helped build, develop, and implement the Human Resources Management System (HRMS) used by the National Guard Bureau (NGB) to track Soldier and civilian data, process orders, manage movement, etc. Subsequently briefed the system at an international conference.
- Army Flight School: flew the TH-67, OH-58, and the UH-1H helicopters.
- Helped test the cockpit of the RAH-66 Comanche Helicopter, designed to fit the smallest to the tallest pilots.
- Original team member on two significant Civil Support Teams (the 45th and the 21st); directly responsible for the initial Federal Certification for Operational Performance (Exit Evaluation (EXEVAL)).
- In charge of the first NGB Operation Warrior Gauntlet, Army Warrior Training in the National Capital Region, from which I received an Army Commendation Medal and Certificate of Achievement from higher headquarter divisions.
- Created and managed the first ARNG administrative SOP for the ARNG Liaison Office at SWCS.
- Instituted and managed the first ARNG promotion board to allow SFQC graduates to better complete requirements for promotion to SSG/E6.
- Created and edited the first Permanent Change of Station (PCS) Guide for ARNG Soldiers arriving for the Special Forces Qualification Course.
- Created and maintained the first ARNG Student Database from scratch leveraging MS Access with User Guide. This system soon replaced the entire system used previously and included an automatic document creation function.
- Completed over 40 static line jumps from various aircraft (C-130, C-141, UH-60, and one ramp jump).
- Received a Certificate of Excellence for scoring 290 and 300 on the Fall 2011 and Spring 2012 (respectively) Army Physical

Fitness Tests.

Military Schools, Training, & Promotions

- **1988**:

  - ○ Basic Training
  - ○ Administrative Specialist Course (AIT)

    - ■ Received *Memorandum for Outstanding Performance* and completed *Fastrack Graduation*

  - ○ Promotion to PV1 in the USAR

- **1989**:

  - ○ Promotion to PV2 in the USAR
  - ○ Equipment Records & Parts Specialist (AIT)

    - ■ Graduated as *Honor Grad*

- ○ Tactical Army Combat Service Support Computer System / Standard Army Maintenance System (TACCS/SAMS) course, only offered to top-performers at AIT

  - ■ Graduated as *Distinguished Honor Grad,* and received AUSA award for Academic Achievement for a perfect score on all tests.

- **1991:**

  - ○ Promotion to SPC on Active Duty

- **1992:**

  - ○ Assigned to 1/507th Infantry (Airborne), Fort Benning, GA

- **1993:**

  - ○ Primary Leadership Development Course

    - ■ *Exceeded Course Standards* by earning a 97% GPA and demonstrating superior communication and leadership skills.

- **1994:**

  - ○ Airborne School

    - ■ Graduated as the *Enlisted Honor Grad*

- **1995:**

  - ○ Promotion to SGT on Active Duty
  - ○ Pathfinder School
  - ○ Combat Lifesaver Course

- **1997:**

- ○ Warrant Officer Candidate School

  - ■ Appointed as a Reserve Warrant Officer on July 3, 1997
- ○ Initial Entry Rotary Wing Course

  - ■ Flew the TH-67, OH-58, and UH-1

- **2001**:

  - ○ Automated Logistical Specialist Course

- **2002**:

  - ○ Assigned to the 45th Civil Support Team (Weapons of Mass Destruction), Smyrna, TN
  - ○ NFPA 472 HAZMAT Technician Course

- **2003**:

  - ○ Promotion to SSG in the ARNG – Title 32
  - ○ Small Scale Production Course
  - ○ Training NCO Course
  - ○ Basic Non-Commission Officer Course (BNCOC) phases 1 and 2

    - ■ *Exceeded Course Standards* and graduated phase 2 as the *Distinguished Honor Grad*, receiving the Coin of Excellence for outstanding achievement.

  - ○ Toxic Agent Training

- **2004**:

  - ○ Assigned to the 21st Civil Support Team (Weapons of Mass Destruction), Fort Dix, NJ
  - ○ Personnel Admin Specialist Course

    - ■ Recognized on the *Commandant's List*

  - ○ Chemical/Biological Survey Course
  - ○ Civil Support Skills Course

- ○ Basic HAPSITE Course
- ○ Consequence Assessment Tools Set with Joint Assessment of Catastrophic Events Course (CATS-JACE) introductory and advanced courses
- ○ Hazardous Materials (HAZMAT) Technician Course
- ○ Basic Hapsite Course
- ○ Combat Lifesaver Course
- ○ HAZMAT General Familiarization / Awareness Training
- ○ Hazard Prediction Assessment Course (HPAC) Level 1
- ○ Counter-Terrorism Intelligence & Awareness Seminar
- ○ Intro to ArcGIS

- **2005**:

  - ○ Promotion to SFC in the ARNG – Title 32

- **2006**:

  - ○ Advanced Non-Commission Officer Course (ANCOC)

    - ■ Recognized for superior participation and leadership skills

  - ○ Assigned to the National Guard Bureau, Arlington, VA

- **2009**:

  - ○ Promotion to MSG in the ARNG – Title 10

- **2012**:

  - ○ Assigned to JFK Special Warfare Center & School, Fort Bragg, NC

Decorations/Badges
The following are listed in order of importance.

- Army Commendation Medal (ARCOM) (x2)
- Award Army Achievement Medal (AAM) (x3)
- Air Force Achievement Medal (AFAM)
- Army Good Conduct Medal (AGCM) (x5)

- National Defense Service Medal (NDSM), with Bronze Service Star Device
- Global War on Terrorism Service Medal (GWTSM)
- Army Service Ribbon
- Army Staff Identification Badge (ASIB)
- Overseas Service Ribbon (OSR)
- Royal Netherlands Army Parachute Badge
- Chilean Parachutist Badge
- Honduran Military Airborne Badge
- French Army Parachutist Badge
- German Armed Forces Parachutist Badge
- Basic Parachutist Badge
- Army Pathfinder Badge
- Superior Unit Award (ASUA) (x3)
- State Armed Forces Reserve Medal (AFRM) (x2)
- Maryland State Service Ribbon (x2)

Road & Trail Races

- **Marathons**

  - New Orleans Rock N Roll Marathon | *New Orleans, LA*
  - Inaugural Raleigh Rock N Roll Marathon | *Raleigh, NC*

- **Half Marathons**

  - Marine Corps Historic Half | *Fredericksburg, VA*
  - Run Like a Diva Half Marathon | *Myrtle Beach, SC*
  - Music City Half Marathon | *Nashville, TN*
  - NC Half Marathon (Charlotte Motor Speedway) | *Concord, NC*
  - Kings Mountain Half Marathon | *Clover, NC*
  - Fort Bragg Mike to Mike Half Marathon | *Fort Bragg, NC*
  - Alexandria Running Festival Half Marathon | *Alexandria, VA*
  - Rock N Roll Las Vegas / *Las Vegas, NV*
  - Rock N Roll USA / *Washington, DC*

- **10-Milers & 10Ks**

  - The Army Ten-Miler | *Arlington, VA* (2x)
  - Cherry Blossom Ten Miler | *Arlington, VA*
  - Marine Corps 10K | *Washington, DC*
  - Joint Special Operations 10K Trail Run | *Fort Bragg, NC*

- **Other**
  - 5k Rebel Race, Frederick, MD
  - 10 Mile Tough Mudder | *Mount Pleasant, NC*

Post-Retirement & Civilian
Significant Achievements & Events

- Lionettes Drill Team, Heidelberg High School, 1985

- Cheerleader, Ramstein Air Force Football Team, 1990

- Established a YouTube channel, @PetitePrincess92, 2006

- Original competitor in the *Ms. Veteran America* competition held in Arlington, VA, 2012

- Joined the American Legion, Post 202, 2017

- Elected to the position of Adjutant for Post 202, Fayetteville, NC, 2018

- Attended the American Legion National Convention in Minneapolis, MN, 2018

- On the cover of the *American Legion National Magazine*, 2018

- Why you should belong brochure, *American Legion*, 2021

- Guest Speaker at a Veterans Day celebration, 2018

- Line Dance Instructor, DC/MD/VA, 2008 – 2012

- Line Dance Instructor Fayetteville, NC, 2016–2020

- Started 2 line dance groups: DMV Fuzion & Fuzion Steppers

- Hosted my first Soul Line Dance party in downtown Fayetteville, NC with over 200 guests

- Chicago Steppin' Instructor at EE Miller Recreation Center and the Retired Military Association (RMA), Fayetteville, NC, 2018

- Joined the Disabled American Veterans (DAV), 2019

- Started a Peer Support Group in Pinehurst, NC, 2018

- Established MSG Erinn Watkins Facebook Page, @MS-GErinnWatkins

- Completed the PGA Hope golf program for Veterans, Franklin, TN, 2022

- Completed the Ladies Golf Clinic, Franklin, TN, 2022

Civilian Schools

- McDonogh 35 Sr High School, New Orleans, LA
- Mu Alpha Theta Math Club 1987
- Mathematics honor society for high school and two-year college students
- Southern University at New Orleans
- Cheerleader
- Excelsior College US

Dance Styles I've Learned

- Chicago Steppin'
- DC Hand Dance
- DC Bop
- Soul Line Dance
- Swing Dance
- Philly Cha Cha
- Two Step & Strand
- Detroit Ballroom
- Salsa
- Cha Cha Cha
- Bachata
- Merengue

Dance Instructor Experience

- **2010:**

    ○ Hillcrest Heights Community Center | Fort Washington, MD
    ○ ROC City Line Dance Extravaganza | Rochester, NY
    ○ Chicago Style Stepping and Soul Line Dancing Event | Silver Spring, MD
    ○ Soulful Saturdays at Weyone Lounge | Alexandria, VA
    ○ "Share My Life" Line Dance Workshop | Suitland, MD
    ○ A Sunday Swing Event for State's Attorney Angela Alsobrooks | Fort Washington, DC
    ○ 1st Annual SE Largest Line Dance Party | Atlanta, GA
    ○ "Steppers on the Move" Line Dance Workshop | Baltimore, MD
    ○ Let's Get Up and Move Fundraiser | Washington, DC

- **2011:**

    ○ 2nd Annual SE Largest Line Dance Party | Atlanta, GA
    ○ Dancing N2 Spring Line Dance Workshop | Sandston, VA
    ○ 105 Voices of History, Howard University Health Fair | Washington, DC

- **2012:**

- ○ Largo Community Church Health Fair | Largo, MD
- ○ United We Dance Soul Line Dance Convention | Indianapolis, IN
- ○ NY Chicago Style Steppers Line Dance Workshop | New York City, NY
- ○ Line Dance Fever & Fitness, Raleigh, NC
- ○ 14th Street Line Dance Crew | Winston-Salem, NC
- ○ Marquis Market Line Dance Class | Fayetteville, NC

- **2013:**

- ○ GDI Line Dance Workshop | Atlanta, GA
- ○ NY Chicago Style Steppers Line Dance Workshop | New York City, NY
- ○ Cool Virginia Steppers | Richmond, VA

- **2014:**

- ○ "Dare 2B Different" Line Dance & Fitness Workshop | Durham, NC
- ○ Line Dance Class at Marquis Market | Fayetteville, NC

- **2015:**

- ○ Line Dance Class at Legendz Sports Bar & Restaurant | Fayetteville, NC
- ○ Line Dance Class at EE Miller Recreation Center | Fayetteville, NC

- **2017:**

- ○ Chicago Stepping Class at Retired Military Association | Fayetteville, NC

PHOTO GALLERY

Basic Training Gas Chamber, Ft Jackson, SC

W Co, Ft Lee, VA

Army Pathfinder Class 6-95, Ft Benning, GA

Promotion to SGT/E5, McCarthy Hall, Ft Benning, GA

NCO of the Month, Ft Benning, GA

Harness Shed, Jump Branch, Ft Benning, GA

Flight School, Ft Rucker, AL

USAJFKSWCS, Ft Bragg, NC

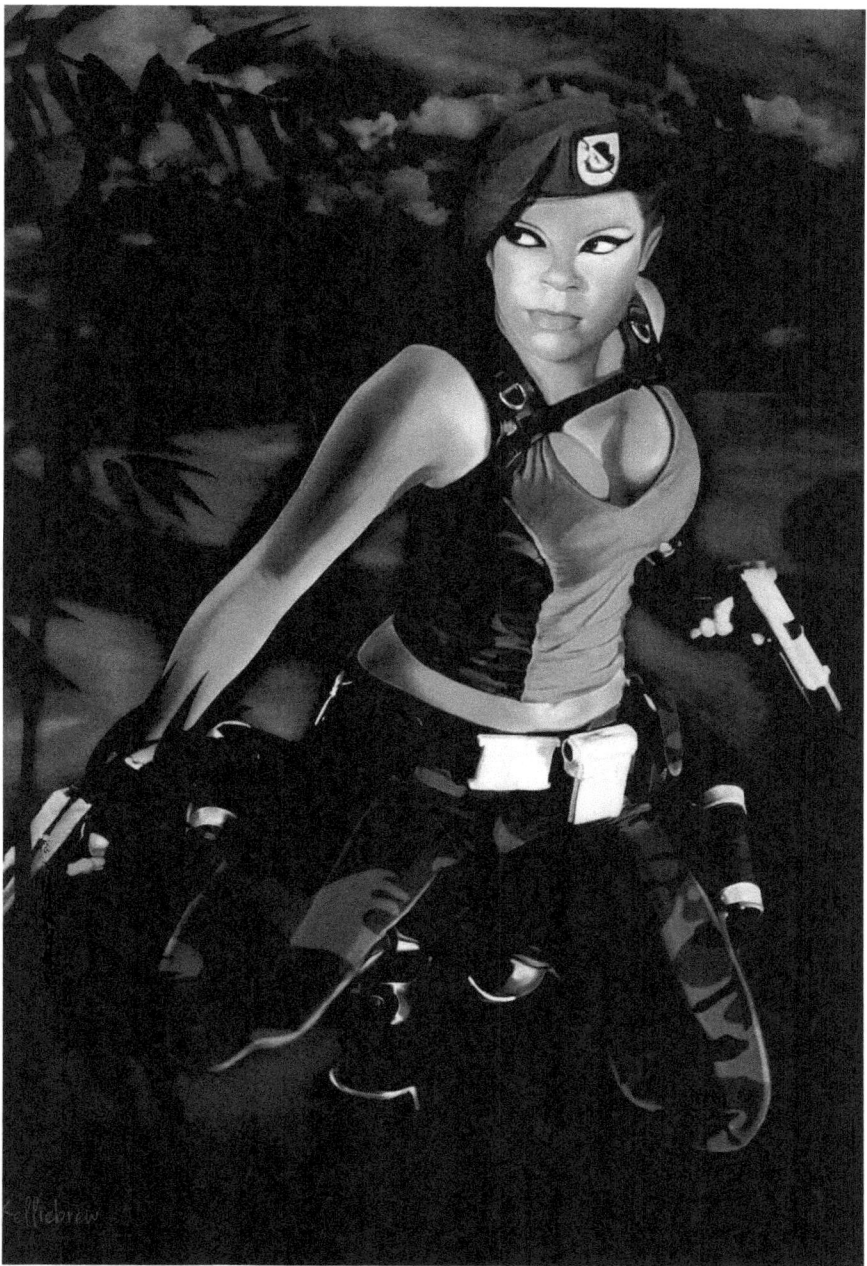

By Kia Kelliebrew

GLOSSARY

- **AIT** – Advanced Individual Training

- **APFT** – Army Physical Fitness Test

- **ArcGIS** – a family of client, server and online geographic information system (GIS) software developed and maintained by Esri

- **ASVAB** – Armed Services Vocational Aptitude Battery

- **Black Hat** – Airborne School Instructor

- **CSM** – Command Sergeant Major/E9, Army rank

- **DMV** – DC, Maryland, Virginia

- **EO** – Equal Opportunity

- **IERW** – Initial Entry Rotary Wing

- **JAG** – Judge Advocate General

- **JFHQ** – Joint Force Headquarters

- **JMPI** – Jumpmaster Personnel Inspection

- **JROTC** – Junior Reserve Officers Training Corps

- **LTC** – Lieutenant Colonel/O5, Army rank

- **MAJ** – Major/O4, Army rank

- **MG** – Major General/O8, Army rank

- **MOS** – Military Occupational Specialty

- **NCO** – Non-Commissioned Officer

- **NCOER** – Non-Commissioned Officer Evaluation Report

- **NCOIC** – Non-Commissioned Officer In-Charge

- **NGB** – National Guard Bureau

- **PLDC** – Primary Leadership Development Course

- **PLF** – Parachute Landing Fall

- **Senior Wings** – Senior Parachutist: Awarded to individuals rated excellent in character and efficiency who have participated in a minimum of 30 jumps to include 15 jumps with combat equipment; two night jumps, one of which is as jumpmaster of a stick; two mass tactical jumps which culminate in an airborne assault problem; graduated from the Jumpmaster Course; and served on jump status with an airborne unit or other organization authorized parachutists for a total of at least 24 months.

- **SFQC** – Special Forces Qualification Course

- **SGI** – Small Group Instructor

- **SGM** – Sergeant Major/E9, Army rank

- **SGT** - Sergeant/E5, Army rank

- **SOP** – Standard Operating Procedures

- **SPC** – Specialist/E4, Army rank

- **SWCS** – Special Warfare Center & School

- **WOCS** – Warrant Officer Candidate School

REFERENCES AND CREDITS

Erinn Speaks
https://erinnspeaks.com

PetitePrincess92
https://www.youtube.com/petiteprincess92

Creating The Queen's Gambit | Netflix
https://www.youtube.com/watch?v=LzDhpEInMIg

Floyd Landis: Tour de France is a war
https://www.youtube.com/watch?v=z_2kAtFfPJ0

Kenneth Johnson
http://www.iamkennyj.com/

Kia Kelliebrew
https://kia-kelliebrew.pixels.com/

Meditation, THE FIRST and LAST FREEDOM, A practical guide to OSHO meditations
https://oshomedia.blog.osho.com/2012/02/osho-meditation-the-first-and-last-freedom/

University of Texas at Austin 2014 Commencement Address - Admiral William H. McRaven
https://youtu.be/pxBQLFLei70

Waypoint Vets
https://waypointvets.org/

Why It's CRITICAL To Detach in Real Time - Jocko Willink and Echo Charles
https://www.youtube.com/watch?v=o5TPO2D6llg

VERDELITE PUBLISHING, LLC

www.verdelitepublishing.com

www.ingramcontent.com/pod-product-compliance
Lightning Source LLC
Chambersburg PA
CBHW060514130626
46553CB00002B/497